A

Minister

Everyone

Would

RESPECT

A Study of 2 Corinthians 8–13

From the Bible-Teaching Ministry of

CHARLES R. SWINDOLL

INSIGHT FOR LIVING

Insight for Living's Bible teacher, Chuck Swindoll, has devoted his life to the clear, practical application of God's Word and His grace. A pastor at heart, Chuck has served as senior pastor to congregations in Texas, Massachusetts, and California. He currently leads Stonebriar Community Church in Frisco, Texas, but Chuck's listening audience extends far beyond a local church body. As a leading program in Christian broadcasting, *Insight for Living* airs in major Christian and non-Christian radio markets throughout the world and to a growing webcast audience. Chuck's extensive writing ministry has also served the body of Christ worldwide, and his leadership as president and now chancellor of Dallas Theological Seminary has helped prepare and equip a new generation for ministry. Chuck and Cynthia, his partner in life and ministry, have four grown children and ten grandchildren.

Based on the outlines and transcripts of Charles R. Swindoll's sermons, in 1989 the Bible study guide was written by Ken Gire, a graduate of Texas Christian University and Dallas Theological Seminary. In 2001 this guide was revised and expanded by the Pastoral Ministries Department of Insight for Living.

Editor in Chief:
Cynthia Swindoll

Study Guide Writer:
Ken Gire

Senior Editor and Assistant Writer:
Marla DeShong

Freelance Writer:
Glenda Schlahta

Editor:
Amy LaFuria

Rights and Permissions:
The Meredith Agency

Text Designer:
Gary Lett

Typesetter:
Bob Haskins

Unless otherwise identified, all Scripture references are from the New American Standard Bible, © The Lockman Foundation 1960, 1962, 1963, 1968, 1971, 1972, 1973, 1975, 1977, 1995. Used by permission. Scripture taken from the Holy Bible, New International Version, Copyright © 1973, 1978, 1984 International Bible Society, used by permission of Zondervan Bible Publishers [NIV]. Other translations cited are the Living Bible [LB] and the Revised Standard Version [RSV].

An effort has been made to locate sources and obtain permission where necessary for the quotations used in this book. In the event of any unintentional omission, a modification will gladly be incorporated in future printings.

ISBN 1-57972-373-X
Cover design: Michael Standlee Design
Cover image: © David P. Hall/Masterfile
Printed in the United States of America

CONTENTS

*This message was not a part of the original series but is compatible with it.

INTRODUCTION

The second letter Paul wrote to the Corinthians is his most autobiographical. From these pages we not only learn a great deal about the qualities of his ministry, we discover the man himself. And what a man he was . . . a minister everyone respected.

In the final six chapters of this letter, Paul unveils many things about his life that are mentioned nowhere else in Scripture. Among these are his convictions regarding financial generosity, the criticism he lived with and hardships he endured, his struggle with "a thorn in the flesh," and even his tender affection for fellow Christians. We want to examine each one carefully. But more importantly, let's commit ourselves to cultivating a similar philosophy of life, because such models are rare today!

I commend you for your diligence to stay with me through the latter half of Second Corinthians. Like me, you are probably realizing how far the church in general and God's people in particular have drifted from the first-century pattern. My prayer is that God will enable us to believe what we discover in His Word and then use what we learn to make a difference in a day like ours when many in ministry have lost their way . . . and others' respect.

Chuck Swindoll

Charles R. Swindoll

PUTTING TRUTH
INTO ACTION

K nowledge apart from application falls short of God's desire for His children. He wants us to apply what we learn so that we will change and grow. This Bible study guide was prepared with these goals in mind. As you go through the following pages, we hope your desire to discover biblical truth will grow as your understanding of God's Word increases and that you will be encouraged to apply what you've learned.

To assist you in your study, we've included a section called **Living Insights** at the end of each lesson. These exercises will challenge you to study further and to think of specific ways to put your discoveries into action.

There are many ways to use this guide—in personal devotions, group studies, discussions with friends and family, and Sunday School classes. And, of course, it's an ideal study aid when you're listening to its corresponding *Insight for Living* radio series.

To benefit most from this Bible study guide, we encourage you to consider it a spiritual journal. That's why we've included space in the **Living Insights** for recording your thoughts and discoveries. We hope you'll return to those sections often for review and encouragement as you continue to grow in your walk with Christ.

Insight for Living

A

Minister

Everyone

Would

RESPECT

A Study of 2 Corinthians 8–13

2 Corinthians: A Man and His Ministry

Writer: Paul
Date: A.D. 54–55
Style: Personal, Bold, Defensive

Uniqueness: This letter seems to be the least systematic of Paul's writing—these are the words of a man who freely expresses his feelings about himself and his ministry.

Introduction and Salutation	Crucial Concerns	Grace Giving	Apostolic Authority	Conclusion and Farewell
	Suffering and God's Sufficiency Ministry and Our Involvement Godliness and Its Impact	Example of Macedonians Command to Corinthians	Reply to Critics Justification of Ministry False Teachers Visions, Revelations, Credentials, Warnings God's Power Perfected in Weakness	
1:1–2	1:3–7:16	8:1–9:15	10:1–13:10	13:11–14

Scope:	Past	Present	Future	
Issues:	Misunderstandings, Concerns, Explanations	Financial Project	Vindication of Paul's Ministry	
Tone:	Forgiving, Grateful, Bold	Confident	Defensive, Strong	
Key verses:	"For we do not preach ourselves but Christ Jesus as Lord." (4:5a)	"God loves a cheerful giver." (9:7b)	"I shall not be put to shame." (10:8b)	

Chapter 1

MAKING GOOD SENSE WITH OUR DOLLARS

2 Corinthians 8:1–9

What item would you say tells the story of your life? Your photo albums? Certainly; they show some of the people you love and the places you've been. Your journals? Of course; they reveal some of your deepest feelings and most private thoughts. But there's one item you may not have thought about: your checkbook.

That's right! Our checkbooks display our lifestyles, our values, and our priorities. They're even a good gauge of our walk with God, because they reflect what our treasures are.

Jesus said a lot about treasure while He was on earth. In fact, one-third of His parables address principles of *stewardship*—how we handle the resources He has entrusted to us. His main concern wasn't money itself, but the condition and motivation of our hearts. As He said in His Sermon on the Mount: "Where your treasure is, there your heart will be also" (Matt. 6:21).

God's Instructions on Giving

One of the most important aspects of being wise stewards of our money is generosity. The Bible instructs us to share with those in need. Deuteronomy 15:8 tells us, "You shall freely open your hand to him, and shall generously lend him sufficient for his need in whatever he lacks." Proverbs 11:25 assures us: "The generous man will be prosperous, And he who waters will himself be watered." And Paul reminds us in 1 Timothy 6:18 that God's people need to "be rich in good works, to be generous and ready to share."

1

Clearly, investing in the lives of others through openhearted giving is an essential part of God's call.

Let's look at what four New Testament passages have to say about giving.

1 Corinthians 9

From this passage, we can formulate the *justification* for giving:

> If we sowed spiritual things in you, is it too much if we should reap material things from you? . . . Do you not know that those who perform sacred services eat the food of the temple, and those who attend regularly to the altar have their share from the altar? So also the Lord directed those who proclaim the gospel to get their living from the gospel. (vv. 11, 13–14)

Paul and his fellow laborers in the faith were making many sacrifices to meet the spiritual needs of the Corinthian believers. Here, Paul reminds them that they have a responsibility to support their spiritual leaders and help provide for their physical and financial needs. In this passage, we also see that remuneration for ministry is specifically sanctioned by God, although Paul chose not to accept payment for his spiritual labor (see vv. 12, 15–18; Acts 20:33–35).

1 Corinthians 16

From this next passage, we can develop *instructions* for giving:

> Now concerning the collection for the saints, as I directed the churches of Galatia, so do you also. On the first day of every week each one of you is to put aside and save, as he may prosper, so that no collections be made when I come. (vv. 1–2)

Paul instructs the Corinthian believers to give according to the following standards:

- Systematically — "on the first day of every week"

- Individually—"let each one of you"

- Consistently—"put aside and save"

- Proportionately—"as he may prosper"

- Privately—"no collections be made when I come"

In these verses we see no pressure, no announcement, no public attention, and no manipulative techniques. How different from the way things often are today! It was understood that the Corinthians would make giving a regular part of their weekly worship.

2 Corinthians 8

This passage, which we will expand on later, offers two *illustrations* of generosity: that of the Macedonians (vv. 1–3) and that of Jesus Christ (v. 9).

2 Corinthians 9

From this passage, we can glean some *applications*:

> He who sows sparingly will also reap sparingly, and he who sows bountifully will also reap bountifully. Each one must do just as he has purposed in his heart, not grudgingly or under compulsion, for God loves a cheerful giver. And God is able to make all grace abound to you, so that always having all sufficiency in everything, you may have an abundance for every good deed; as it is written,
> "He scattered abroad, he gave to the poor,
> His righteousness endures forever."
> (vv. 6–9; see also Ps. 112)

Giving is not intended to be done simply as a duty or an obligation. Joyful giving is a matter of the heart!

Paul's Encouragement to Give

To understand Paul's comments in chapters 8 and 9 regarding giving, it's important to understand the context in which these remarks were made. The church in Jerusalem was experiencing extreme financial need due to the immense number of converts from the day of Pentecost as well as outbreaks of famine during the reign of the emperor Claudius (A.D. 41-54).

Despite their own financial woes, the churches in Macedonia rose to the occasion, giving generously and sacrificially. The Macedonian Christians were not only extremely poor, but they had also endured a great deal of persecution.[1] Still, Paul tells the Corinthians:

> Now, brethren, we wish to make known to you
> the grace of God which has been given in the
> churches of Macedonia, that in a great ordeal of
> affliction their abundance of joy and their deep pov-
> erty overflowed in the wealth of their liberality.
> (2 Cor. 8:1–2)

Not only did the Macedonian believers give generously, but they also gave voluntarily. Paul notes in verse 3:

> For I testify that according to their ability, and be-
> yond their ability, they gave of their own accord.

The Macedonians gave willingly, with no prompting or pressure from Paul. In fact, they even pleaded with Paul and Titus to take their money—as Paul says, "begging us with much urging for the favor of participation in the support of the saints" (v. 4).

These believers didn't regard giving as an obligation, but a privilege. Paul's words tell us where this attitude came from:

> They first gave themselves to the Lord and to us by
> the will of God. (v. 5b)

Good stewards have willing hearts. When we give ourselves fully to the Lord, we want to heap our time, our talents, and our treasure at His feet. Nothing matters to us as much as His cause and His people. If we find ourselves clutching our possessions with a tight fist, the problem probably goes deeper than our wallets.

A Reminder to the Corinthians

The Corinthians had given generously of their resources a year or so earlier. But their initial enthusiasm had waned, and they had not followed through on their pledge of support. In verse 6, Paul encourages them to complete their giving:

> So we urged Titus that as he had previously made a
> beginning, so he would also complete in you this
> gracious work as well.

1. Colin G. Kruse, "2 Corinthians," in *New Bible Commentary: 21st Century Edition*, 4th ed., rev., gen. eds. D.A. Carson, R.T. France, J.A. Motyer, and G. J. Wenham (Downer's Grove, Ill.: InterVarsity Press, 1994), p. 1199.

Unlike the Macedonians, the Corinthians were flourishing financially. They had plenty of resources, yet their giving had not continued. Paul gives them a gentle prod in the next verse:

> But just as you abound in everything, in faith and utterance and knowledge and in all earnestness and in the love we inspired in you, see that you abound in this gracious work also. (v. 7)

Paul begins by reminding the Corinthians of their blessings and commending them on the spiritual fruit he sees them producing. But he goes on to urge them to develop in the area of giving as well.

Think about your own stewardship habits for a moment. Perhaps you are committed to Bible study. Maybe you devote yourself to prayer, evangelism, and serving others. Wonderful! But are you also consistent in your giving? The margins of your Bible may be crowded with notes, but if your checkbook contains only notations to department stores and credit card companies, it may be an indication that your spiritual life is out of balance.

The Example of Christ

Paul is quick to point out that he is not *demanding* that the Corinthians give. He simply reminds them that the grace and sacrificial love that Jesus showed them should motivate them to give to others:

> I am not speaking this as a command, but as proving through the earnestness of others the sincerity of your love also. For you know the grace of our Lord Jesus Christ, that though He was rich, yet for your sake He became poor, so that you through His poverty might become rich. (vv. 8–9)

Notice the subtle contrast. Though the Macedonians were poor, they gave as though they were rich. Though Jesus was rich, He lived as if He were poor. Paul notes in his letter to the Philippians:

> Although He existed in the form of God, [He] did not regard equality with God a thing to be grasped, but emptied Himself, taking the form of a bond-servant, and being made in the likeness of men. Being found in appearance as a man, He humbled

Himself by becoming obedient to the point of death,
even death on a cross. (Phil. 2:6–8)

Putting the Truth to Work

How can we apply this study of generous giving to our daily
lives? Let's highlight two important aspects:

First: *Claiming God's grace without receiving God's Son is impossible.*
God's grace is only available to us through the gift of His Son, Jesus
Christ. We who have established a personal relationship with Christ
are expected to give of our resources willingly, just as Jesus sacrificed
all that He had for us. Even when times are hard, God promises to
provide for all of our needs if we continue to trust Him and give.

Second: *Walking in grace without giving our treasure is incomplete.*
Everything we own has been given to us by God to be used for His
purposes. God certainly does not *need* our financial help. But He
allows us the *privilege* of participating in His work through our
giving. When we don't want to give to help others, it says something
about the state of our hearts.

Living Insights

Let's get personal for a moment. Looking back over the last year
or so, would you say your financial situation has been more like
that of the Macedonians or the Corinthians?

_____

_____

Now think about your giving pattern. Does it more closely
resemble the Macedonians' or the Corinthians'?

_____

_____

If your giving has been like that of the Macedonians, list the
things that motivate your generosity.

_____

_____

_____

_____

If your giving has been more like that of the Corinthians, write down the things that tend to get in the way of more generous giving.

_____

_____

_____

If you have trouble parting with your treasure, you may be having a hard time trusting God with your needs. Or you might fully intend to give each month, but undisciplined spending causes you to wind up with empty pockets. Examine your heart now and ask God to show you the areas in your financial life where you need to let go and trust Him. List them here.

_____

_____

_____

_____

_____

Seek God's wisdom concerning the investment of your treasure. Remember what Jesus said in Matthew 6:21: "Where your treasure is, there your heart will be also."

Chapter 2

FANNING THE FINANCIAL FIRE
2 Corinthians 8:10–24

Most of us agree that money can't buy happiness—but wouldn't we like to try it and see? As Irish poet, playwright, and wit Oscar Wilde wrote, "Young people, nowadays, imagine that money is everything . . . and when they grow older they know it!"[1] Or as former heavyweight champ Joe Louis said, "I don't like money, actually, but it quiets my nerves."[2]

Too often, we put our trust in our money, holding tightly to it for fear of losing our security or some measure of control over our lives. We feel that we have the right to do whatever we want with it—we earned it, and we can spend it as we please. After all, it's *ours*, isn't it?

Well, not completely. Let's gather some clues from Scripture that will help us understand that God is the provider of all our resources. We will also gain insight into the problems that the Corinthians needed to confront.

Four Words That Will Open Our Hands

Four simple words can help us keep our money in perspective: *God owns it all*. Let's see what the Bible has to say about money in the following passages:

> "Whatever is under the whole heaven is Mine." (Job. 41:11b)

> "All the earth is Mine." (Exod. 19:5b)

> The earth is the Lord's, and everything in it,
>   the world, and all who live in it. (Ps. 24:1 NIV)

> You are not your own. . . . You were bought with a price. (1 Cor. 6:19b; 7:23a)

> We have brought nothing into the world, so we cannot take anything out of it either. (1 Tim. 6:7)

1. Oscar Wilde, *The Picture of Dorian Gray and Selected Stories* (New York, N.Y.: Penguin Books, Signet Classic, 1983), p. 48.

2. Joe Louis, at http://www.geocities.com/~spanoudi/quote-6b.html, accessed on July 25, 2001.

All that we have, all that we think we own, is really God's. We were born with empty hands, and we'll leave this world that way, too. God owns it *all*. We must remember that we are stewards, not owners, of the possessions God has given us.

The Corinthians may have confused the two, regarding their money as their own property rather than a resource God had entrusted to them to help his people. Read on to see how Paul wisely set the matter straight and helped these believers open their hearts and hands for God's glory.

Paul's Wise and Gentle Advice

A year earlier, moved by the plight of the church in Jerusalem, Christians in Corinth had begun a giving project to help their sister church. With the passage of time, though, their enthusiasm had waned, and their contributions had dwindled to nothing—yet the financial needs in Jerusalem were as desperate as ever. So Paul writes to encourage the Corinthians to complete their giving project.

Three Incentives

Paul reminded the Corinthian believers of three things. First, *stop and consider the blessings of God*. The Corinthians abounded in "everything" (2 Cor. 8:7). They had faith, good teaching, knowledge, earnestness, and love—and we can gather that they were quite blessed financially. When we are grateful for what we have rather than dwelling on the things we don't have, generosity tends to come more easily.

Second, *listen to the testimony of others* (v. 8). Paul wanted the Corinthians to consider the earnest, abundant gifts that the Macedonian believers had given despite their own hardship and lack of material wealth. He urged the Corinthians to follow the example of the Macedonian churches.

Third, *look at the example of Christ* (v. 9). Though Christ could have had all the world's riches, He chose to live like a pauper. And He did it out of love—a self-sacrificing, joy-focused, running-over kind of love that rescues us from spiritual poverty and freely offers us God's riches. When we reflect on Christ's immense grace, we can't help but be moved to extend grace to others.

Four Hindrances

It seems like these incentives would be enough, doesn't it? But

9

our human nature can be tough to change. Like us, the Corinthians might have been motivated to give on Sunday morning, but come Monday . . . well, the urge had passed. What happened?

In Paul's words to the slow-to-give Corinthians, we can find four hindrances to giving. The first is *procrastination*:

> I give my opinion in this matter, for this is to your advantage, who were the first to begin a year ago not only to do this, but also to desire to do it. But now finish doing it also. (vv. 10–11a)

The dictionary defines *procrastinate* as "to put off intentionally and habitually . . . the doing of something that should be done."[3] Procrastination has also been called "the art of keeping up with yesterday."[4] The procrastinator's favorite word? *Tomorrow.* "Tomorrow I'll get organized . . . tomorrow I'll go on a diet . . . tomorrow I'll start giving to the poor." But for the procrastinator, tomorrow never comes. The only way to break the cycle is, as Paul said, to do it *now*.

The second hindrance is closely related to the first: *hesitation*. Hesitation says, "I'm just not ready." But Paul knew the Corinthians were ready and willing, so he encouraged them to put their desire into action:

> Just as there was the readiness to desire it, so there may be also the completion of it by your ability. For if the readiness is present, it is acceptable according to what a person has, not according to what he does not have. (vv. 11b–12)

Did you catch Paul's liberating message in verse 12? If we're eager, motivated, enthusiastic, and excited about giving, then God will bless whatever we can afford to give; we don't need to feel ashamed if we can't give as much as the next person.

That feeling of inadequacy is at the heart of the third hindrance: *overreaction*.

> For if the readiness is present, it is acceptable according to what a person has, not according to what he does not have. (v. 12)

---

3. *Merriam-Webster's Collegiate Dictionary*, 10th ed., see "procrastinate."

4. Don Marquis, *archy and mehitobel* (1930; reprint, New York, N.Y.: Doubleday, Anchor Books, 1990), p. 54.

This verse ties in with the last three words of verse 11: "by your ability." We *all* have the ability to give, but the person who over-reacts says, "I don't have much to give; it would hardly be a drop in the bucket. Might as well not do it at all." However, Paul stresses that the amount we give is not as important as having an open-handed attitude toward giving.

Someone else will always be able to give more than we can. And the need will always be greater than our ability to give. But that's not the issue. Paul reminds us here that God doesn't evaluate our gifts by their amount, but by our motives. Remember the story of the poor widow in Mark 12? She's a beautiful illustration of this point:

> And [Jesus] sat down opposite the treasury, and began observing how the people were putting money into the treasury; and many rich people were putting in large sums. A poor widow came and put in two small copper coins, which amount to a cent. Calling His disciples to Him, He said to them, "Truly I say to you, this poor widow put in more than all the contributors to the treasury; for they all put in out of their surplus, but she, out of her poverty, put in all she owned, all she had to live on." (vv. 41–44)

Jesus teaches His disciples an important lesson here—He emphasizes that the motivation for giving is more crucial than the amount. If we remember that all we have has come from God, and if we trust Him to supply our needs, our hands will be more ready to extend joyful generosity to others.

The fourth hindrance can be called *exception*. We know that God wants everyone to be involved in giving—but sometimes we think we might be the exception to His plan. After all, others have more than we do, or we may be going through a tough time. Does God want to impoverish us to make others rich?

Paul's next words reassure us that God's not trying to drain us dry:

> For this is not for the ease of others and for your affliction, but by way of equality—at this present time your abundance being a supply for their need, so that their abundance also may become a supply for your need, that there may be equality; as it is written, "He who gathered much did not have too much, and he who gathered little had no lack" (2 Cor. 8:13–15).

Does Paul mean that all Christians should have the same amount of money? Commentator Paul Barnett offers us some valuable clarification on this passage:

> He does not mean exact *material* equality as in an enforced *per capita* method of contributing which would reduce everyone to the same economic basis. . . . If it is "by force" it cannot be "by grace." According to the varying resources of each, there should be an equal *willingness* to give so that one brother does not coast along at the expense of the too-great sacrifice of another. . . .
>
> Paul illustrates his principle of *equality* or spiritual fairness by the quotation from Exodus 16:18 which refers to the Lord's provision of manna in the wilderness. By God's miraculous working, those who had little and those who had plenty *both* had sufficient. Paul's point is that wherever God's people, however well or poorly endowed, are prepared to use their gifts and money willingly, there will be *equality;* there will be no injustice. Some may have more and others less, but all will have enough.[5]

God has a way of balancing out our possessions to meet needs. The church in Jerusalem needed assistance from the Corinthians, but there could come a time when the burden would shift and the Corinthians might need the help of other believers.

Two Principles

From Paul's next words, we can glean two principles relating to who should handle money and how.

First, *only qualified people should handle financial matters.* Paul wrote to the Corinthians:

> But thanks be to God who puts the same earnestness on your behalf in the heart of Titus. For he not only accepted our appeal, but being himself very earnest, he has gone to you of his own accord. We have sent along with him the brother whose fame

5. Paul Barnett, *The Message of 2 Corinthians: Power in Weakness,* The Bible Speaks Today Series (Downers Grove, Ill.: InterVarsity Press, 1988), p. 146.

in the things of the gospel has spread through all the churches; and not only this, but he has also been appointed by the churches to travel with us in this gracious work, which is being administered by us for the glory of the Lord Himself, and to show our readiness . . . We have sent with them our brother, whom we have often tested and found diligent in many things, but now even more diligent because of his great confidence in you. As for Titus, he is my partner and fellow worker among you; as for our brethren, they are messengers of the churches, a glory to Christ. (1 Cor. 8:16–19, 22–23)

Paul was sending three men—Titus and two unnamed brothers—to collect the money the Corinthians would give for the Jerusalem church. Did you notice their list of credentials? They possessed earnestness (v. 16); appointment by the churches (v. 19); and diligence (v. 22). They were known as partners and fellow workers in the faith (v. 23) and a glory to Christ (v. 23). It's clear that handling financial contributions is not a task for just anyone who volunteers.

The second principle is this: *money matters should be administered honestly and openly.*

This gracious work . . . is being administered by us for the glory of the Lord Himself, and to show our readiness, taking precaution so that no one will discredit us in our administration of this generous gift; for we have regard for what is honorable, not only in the sight of the Lord, but also in the sight of men. (vv. 19b–21)

When people give their money to churches, ministries, and charities, they trust that their money will be used wisely and carefully. That trust is just as valuable as the money—maybe even more—so it must be guarded. We're accountable not only to God, but also to the people who contribute to His work. It's a matter of honor.

In the last verse of the chapter, Paul turns his attention back to the Corinthians, encouraging them to show their love by completing their gift:

Therefore openly before the churches, show them the proof of your love and of our reason for boasting about you. (v. 24)

From Corinth to Our World

Are you in a position to give generously? Or do you find yourself in as much need as those receiving the collection? Whatever your situation, probe your heart with the following five questions to uncover your attitudes toward giving:

1. Do I really believe God owns it all?

2. Have I recently considered God's blessings?

3. Am I currently hiding behind excuses?

4. Can I honestly say I'm convinced of the integrity of the ministries I support?

5. Am I diligent about keeping money from becoming an idol in my life?

 Living Insights

Now answer these questions in depth, allowing them to reveal your attitudes toward giving.

Do I really believe God owns it all? What things in my life are hardest for me to relinquish to God?

_____

_____

_____

_____

_____

Have I recently considered God's blessings? I am thankful for the following blessings I have received from God's hand:

_____

_____

_____

_____

_____

_____

Am I currently hiding behind excuses? What are the reasons I use for not giving at a greater level?

_____

_____

_____

_____

_____

Are these reasons in line with what Paul says about giving? What can I do to get rid of any invalid excuses and improve my attitude toward giving?

_____

_____

_____

_____

_____

Can I honestly say I'm convinced of the integrity of the ministries I support? What do I consider to be the benchmarks of a ministry's integrity? Do the ministries I support fit these criteria?

_____

_____

_____

_____

_____

Am I diligent about keeping money from becoming an idol in my life? Am I consumed by financial worries or the desire for more money or material possessions? What steps can I take to ensure that the pursuit of God—not money—directs my life?

_____

_____

_____

_____

_____

_____

Spend an hour reviewing your checkbook, bank statements, and credit card bills. Ask yourself these questions: Where am I investing my money? How can I redirect my treasure to match God's priorities? What changes can I make in my spending habits to enable me to be a better steward?

_____

_____

_____

_____

_____

_____

Chapter 3

THE TRIP TO
BOUNTIFUL GIVING

2 Corinthians 9:1–6

The setting is the lobby of The Peabody Hotel in Orlando, Florida. The theme song is John Philip Sousa's "Stars and Stripes Forever." The stage is a strip of red carpeting across the main floor, and the performers are a flock of web-footed, high-stepping, orange-billed ducks. They rally their troops at the fountain, then march out in a straight line to the delighted applause of hotel guests, twice a day. It's The Peabody's Parade of Ducks!

How in the world do you get a flock of ducks to step in time across a hotel lobby? Twice a day, no less?

The answer is waiting backstage — food. The ducks don't care about performing. They aren't concentrating on keeping in step or on the red carpet or even on the applause. Their minds are on what's behind the curtain. They know waddling across that lobby is the only way they're going to get fed, so they're willing to waddle.

When it comes to getting a big job done, humans aren't so different from those ducks. Certain ingredients are vital to accomplishing a specific goal. Before we rejoin the Corinthians, let's take a moment to understand what motivates people to accomplish great things.

The Essential Ingredients of Accomplishment

The Corinthians were struggling to finish the giving project that they had started. It's human nature to be overwhelmed just thinking about a big project that needs to be accomplished, especially if we're responsible for completing it. No matter how big the task, though, we can usually break it down into four essential components that will make it easier to achieve.

First, *there must be active participants*. When we face a monumental task, it's no time to isolate ourselves from those around us. It's time to call in the troops—people who will take an active part in helping us.

Second, *there must be clear objectives*. If we don't know where we're going, we certainly won't have any idea about how to get

17

there. Clear goals and objectives provide the needed signposts to our destination.

Third, *there must be strong enthusiasm*. Enthusiasm puts the fun and excitement in any job. Without it, workers soon lose interest and motivation.

Fourth, *there must be the promise of reward*. Tangible rewards fuel the fire of determination and keep us marching toward our goal. However, we find it difficult to maintain our pace and enthusiasm without a leader—someone whose example we can follow. We need someone to motivate, encourage, and reward us.

Paul provided just such gifted leadership to the Corinthians. We can glean some important principles from his encouraging words in 2 Corinthians 9.

The Equation of Generosity

From Paul's appeal to the Corinthians, we can construct an equation of generosity made up of four components.

The Equation Implied

In the first two verses of chapter 9, Paul gives encouragement to the Corinthians through his confidence in them:

> For it is superfluous for me to write to you about this ministry to the saints; for I know your readiness, of which I boast about you to the Macedonians, namely, that Achaia has been prepared since last year, and your zeal has stirred up most of them.

The word *superfluous* means "extra, not needed, unnecessary."[1] Paul knows that the ingredients for accomplishing the task are already in place—the Corinthians have been ready to give for a year now. So Paul communicates how proud of them he is and what a positive impact they've had on others.

From between the lines of his words we can formulate this equation:

(The Right People + The Right Objectives) x (Direction + Enthusiasm) = Accomplishment of the Goal!

1. *Merriam-Webster's Collegiate Dictionary*, 10th ed., see "superfluous."

The believers at Corinth were the right people, and their desire to help the hurting saints in Jerusalem was the right objective. With Paul lending direction to their enthusiasm, they were now sure to accomplish their goal of generous giving.

In verse 2, Paul gives the Corinthians a warm pat on the back to express his confidence in them. Not only that, but he brags about their enthusiasm to the Macedonians. We can get a lot done for the Lord if we'll learn from Paul's positive, uplifting leadership style.

The Equation Explained

In verse 3, Paul explains why he sent Titus and the two other brothers to help the Corinthians complete their project:

> But I have sent the brethren, in order that our boasting about you may not be made empty in this case, so that, as I was saying, you may be prepared.

Notice again that Paul has been "boasting" about them. If you recall from other studies, he had plenty of reasons to complain about them as well! But one of Paul's great qualities was that he apparently never criticized one church to another. When he found something that needed to be addressed and corrected, he dealt only with that person or that church. But when he found something praiseworthy, he affirmed it both privately and publicly. Affirmation makes a profound impact on people.

Paul also wants the Corinthians to live up to his boasting so that all of them will maintain their integrity:

> Otherwise if any Macedonians come with me and find you unprepared, we—not to speak of you—will be put to shame by this confidence. (v. 4)

In essence, Paul is saying, "Look, guys. I've been telling the Macedonians what kind of people you are—generous, enthusiastic, and willing to give. Can you imagine how I'm going to feel if I have to look them in the eye and tell you they didn't get around to taking the collection? Not to mention how embarrassed you're going to be!"

Instead, Paul wants their generosity to shine brightly:

> So I thought it necessary to urge the brethren that they would go on ahead to you and arrange beforehand your previously promised bountiful gift, so that

the same would be ready as a bountiful gift and not
affected by covetousness. (v. 5)

Titus and the other brothers in the faith were coming ahead of
Paul to help the Corinthians make their generous desires a reality.
That way, when Paul and possibly some of the Macedonians came
through Corinth on their way to Jerusalem deliver the gift, "no
collections would have to be made . . . under pressure which
might resemble exploitation."[2] If they waited until the last minute
to collect the money for the gift, it might look like they really didn't
want to give at all.

The Equation Illustrated

In verse 6, Paul shifts from his specific message to the Corinthians to a general message for everyone:

Now this I say, he who sows sparingly will also
reap sparingly, and he who sows bountifully will also
reap bountifully.

Now that's a principle to remember! But it's also one that's been
given a lot of false advertising in recent years. God never promises
to match us dollar for dollar, or even to reward us in kind. What
He promises are the blessings of the heart—the joy of knowing
we're obedient, the pleasure of peace, and the fulfillment of having
a part in His work.

Practical Steps of Involvement

The Corinthians were involved in a project important enough
to be described in Scripture. We, too, have opportunities for involvement. How can we make the most of them? When it comes
to approaching a big project, we can "get our ducks in a row" by
adding up the equation of generosity.

First, *become an active participant*. Move out of the realm of
theory and get into the realm of action. Stop studying about giving,
and start giving! Set goals for yourself, and ask a friend or family
member to help you stay accountable to them.

---

2. David K. Lowery, "2 Corinthians," in *The Bible Knowledge Commentary*, New Testament
edition, ed. John F. Walvoord and Roy B. Zuck (Wheaton, Ill.: SP Publications, Inc., Victor
Books, 1983), p. 575.

Second, *understand the stated objectives*. God makes His guidelines for giving quite clear throughout Scripture. He begins in the Old Testament with the idea of the tithe—giving ten percent of our income to the Lord. Search out the principles available to you in God's Word for help with your giving decisions and goals. (See Matthew 6:2, Luke 6:38, Acts 20:35, and Philippians 4:15.)

Third, *demonstrate strong enthusiasm*. Don't give grudgingly— give with enthusiasm! It's contagious!

Fourth, *remember the promised rewards*. God will honor us for our active, enthusiastic, knowledgeable involvement in His work. He promises to reward and bless us for giving our financial resources to support His causes.

As you consider applying these guidelines to your own life, take some time to consider how Christ demonstrated them while He was on earth. He was an active participant in the mission of salvation; He never lost sight of His goal; He spread enthusiasm for His cause. And the reward? Every day, people come to know and believe in Him "who for the joy set before Him endured the cross, despising the shame, and has sat down at the right hand of the throne of God" (Heb. 12:2b).

Paul's principles apply to all of us. How are you fitting them into your life?

 Living Insights

Are you active in ministry projects that involve giving? Take another look at the four steps of involvement that you've just studied. How do you measure up?

_____

_____

_____

Think of the projects your church is currently involved in that require funding, and choose the one that most interests you. Maybe it's a building effort, ministry to a special group, or the support of a missionary. Whatever it is, write it down here.

_____

_____

_____

Remember the four essential ingredients of accomplishment on pages 17–18? Ask yourself the following questions to help determine your strengths and weaknesses when it comes to your involvement in the project.

To what extent am I an active *participant*? What can I do to become more actively involved in the project?

_____

_____

_____

Do I clearly understand the stated *objectives*? What are they?

_____

_____

_____

Am I demonstrating strong *enthusiasm* for the project? If not, what steps can I take to be a more enthusiastic participant?

_____

_____

_____

Do I keep in mind the *goal* and the *promised rewards*? What are they?

_____

_____

_____

If you aren't currently involved in a ministry project, get involved! If you don't know of any projects or ministries that need help, ask! You just might be God's answer to prayer for that particular ministry. Give generously of your time, effort, and money. Remember—you're investing in eternity!

Chapter 4

GIVING BY GRACE

2 Corinthians 9:6–15

Amazing grace! How sweet the sound,
That saved a wretch like me![1]

You know the song, but do you know the story of the man who wrote it?

John Newton was only seven years old when his godly mother died. He was turned over to relatives and soon forgot the Scriptures she had taught him. By the time he became an apprentice seaman, he had acquired knowledge of a different kind—along with a reputation for being able to curse for two hours straight without repeating a single word!

Later, he joined the British navy, but he couldn't tolerate the discipline required and soon deserted, fleeing to Africa so that, in his own words, "I might sin my fill." Eventually, however, he fell into the hands of a Portuguese slave trader. For months, the chief woman of the trader's harem treated him like an animal, beating him and forcing him to grovel in the dirt for his food.

Finally, emaciated and angry, Newton escaped and found his way to the shores of Africa, where he was picked up by a passing ship. Because he was a skilled navigator, he earned the position of first mate. But while the captain was ashore one day, Newton brought out the ship's rum and got the entire crew drunk. When the captain came back, he was so incensed that he struck Newton, knocking him overboard.

Newton would have drowned were it not for another drunken sailor. The seaman pulled him back on board by spearing Newton's thigh with a boat hook, leaving an enormous wound.

Some weeks later, when the ship neared the coast of Scotland, it sailed into a storm and almost sank. Newton stood manning the pumps—seasick, vomiting, and fearing for his life. In the midst of that terrible storm, Newton was desperate enough to cry out to God. And God miraculously spared his life and changed his heart that day.

---

1. John Newton, "Amazing Grace" in *The Hymnal for Worship and Celebration* (Waco, Tex.: Word Music, 1986), no. 202.

John Newton emerged from that experience to become chaplain to England's Parliament. He even preached before the king! Despite his vile past, this man would later be called by many the second founder of the Church of England. And it was he who wrote these soul-stirring words:

> I once was lost, but now am found,
> Was blind, but now I see.[2]

A Few Thoughts on Grace

Few people could be less deserving of grace than John Newton— or more in need of it. Legalism would have demanded penance of him. But grace never reads the laundry list of our sins. It doesn't point the finger of accusation. Grace comes to us as we are. It accepts us in our ugliness, wretchedness, and desperation. Grace truly is amazing!

Consider these truths about grace. First, *grace stoops to where we are and lifts us to where God is*. Donald Barnhouse had a wonderful way of putting it:

> Love that goes upward is worship; love that goes outward is affection; love that stoops is grace.[3]

David, too, understood grace. He described it poetically in Psalm 40:

> I waited patiently for the Lord;
> And He inclined to me and heard my cry.
> He brought me up out of the pit of destruction,
>   out of the miry clay,
> And he set my feet upon a rock making my footsteps
>   firm.
> He put a new song in my mouth, a song of praise
>   to our God;
> Many will see and fear
> And will trust in the Lord. (Ps. 40:1–3)

---

2. John Newton, "Amazing Grace."

3. Donald Grey Barnhouse, *Man's Ruin: Expositions of Bible Doctrines Taking the Epistle to the Romans as a Point of Departure*, vol. 1 (Grand Rapids, Mich.: William B. Eerdmans Publishing Company, 1952), p. 72.

Grace bends to where we are, reaches into the pit of our wretchedness, lifts us out, and sets us on level ground before God—as righteous as His own Son. Can anything be more amazing than that?

Second, *grace softens the harsh demands of the Law and offers us hope to go on.* Remember the story in John 8:1–11 of the woman caught in adultery? The disheveled, frightened woman was dragged to Jesus by the self-righteous religious leaders. They stood with stones in their hands, ready to kill her—and trying to set a trap for Jesus at the same time. Would He uphold the Law given by the One He claimed had sent Him? Or would He extend the grace He said He came to proclaim?

Jesus shrugged off the scheme, telling the men:

> "He who is without sin among you, let him be the first to throw a stone at her." . . . When they heard it, they began to go out one by one, beginning with the older ones, and He was left alone, and the woman, where she was, in the center of the court. (vv. 7b–9)

The woman slipped free of the cloak of condemnation with Jesus' next words:

> "Woman, where are they? Did no one condemn you?" She said, "No one, Lord." And Jesus said, "I do not condemn you either. Go. From now on sin no more." (vv. 10–11)

Not only did Jesus' words save the life of this woman, but His forgiveness gave her the courage to go on, despite her disgrace. It gave her the motivation to change her life.

Third, *grace becomes our guide in responding to God and others.* Grace is always greater than our own resources, our own pain, our own need—even our own sin:

> "Come now, and let us reason together,"
> Says the Lord,
> "Though your sins are as scarlet,
> They will be as white as snow;
> Though they are red like crimson,
> They will be like wool." (Isa. 1:18)

As He has forgiven us, so He wants us to forgive others:

"Be merciful, just as your Father is merciful."
(Luke 6:36)

Be kind to one another, tender-hearted, forgiving each
other, just as God in Christ also has forgiven you.
Therefore be imitators of God, as beloved children; and walk in love, just as Christ also loved you.
(Eph. 4:32-5:2a; see also Luke 7:36–47)

When we have experienced grace, we can give grace to others.

Specific Applications of Grace

Almost as amazing as God's grace is the astonishing fact that
most people don't respond to it—especially when it comes to giving. But grace is a vital part of financial stewardship that Paul
addresses in his message.

Bountiful Sowing

Paul starts out by using a farming metaphor to illustrate a spiritual truth:

Now this I say, he who sows sparingly will also
reap sparingly, and he who sows bountifully will also
reap bountifully. (2 Cor. 9:6)

Scant sowing makes for scant harvest. Generous sowing, however, makes for an abundant harvest. This thought did not originate
with Paul. In fact, as a Jewish scholar, he would certainly have been
familiar with two verses from Proverbs that give a similar message:

It is possible to give away and become richer! It is
also possible to hold on too tightly and lose everything. (Prov. 11:24 LB)

He who is generous will be blessed. (22:9a)

Even Jesus Himself had spoken on the subject:

"Give, and it will be given to you. They will pour
into your lap a good measure—pressed down,
shaken together, and running over. For by your standard of measure it will be measured to you in return."
(Luke 6:38)

It's important to keep in mind, though, that neither Jesus nor

Paul nor the writer of Proverbs was promising a check in the mailbox on Monday in exchange for a check in the offering plate on Sunday. God's blessings sometimes take surprising forms, but they will always be in line with our needs.

Cheerful Giving

Next, Paul takes the general principle of verse 6 and makes it personal:

> Each one must do just as he has purposed in his heart, not grudgingly or under compulsion, for God loves a cheerful giver. (2 Cor. 9:7)

The Greek term for *purposed* means to "choose beforehand, to decide ahead of time." Doesn't sound like impulse giving, does it? Nor should it originate from external pressures. It should come from within, from the heart. Gracious, cheerful giving is the result of heartfelt, thoughtful resolve. God is much less interested in our money than in the state of our hearts.

Liberal Providing

Having shifted the focus from the Corinthians to the ultimate Giver, God, Paul further elaborates on the lavishness and generous purposes of God's giving:

> And God is able to make all grace abound to you, so that always having all sufficiency in everything, you may have an abundance for every good deed; as it is written,
> "He scattered abroad, he gave to the poor,
> His righteousness abides forever."
> Now He who supplies seed to the sower and bread for food will supply and multiply your seed for sowing and increase the harvest of your righteousness; you will be enriched in everything for all liberality, which through us is producing thanksgiving to God. (vv. 8–11)

It's hard to give when we are struggling financially. But even our most meager gifts unleash the storehouse of God's abundance. Always remember, God doesn't need our money! He owns everything. Giving is about much more than gifts—it offers us the chance to participate in God's work and to become unselfish, generous, and others-centered. It provides us with the opportunity to trust in God for our own needs. It allows us to appreciate God's bounty lavished on us and encourages us to share it with others.

Joyful Response

In verses 12–14, Paul encourages the Corinthians by showing how far-reaching the blessings of giving can be:

> For the ministry of this service is not only fully supplying the needs of the saints, but is also over-flowing through many thanksgivings to God. Because of the proof given by this ministry, they will glorify God for your obedience to your confession of the gospel of Christ and for the liberality of your contribution to them and to all, while they also, by prayer on your behalf, yearn for you because of the surpassing grace of God in you.

Those who give graciously not only meet the real needs of other people, but also bring praise and glory to God. Selfless giving reaches far beyond the immediate needs of the receiver and encourages all of Christ's people who hear of it!

Amazing grace. Abounding grace. Those who give by grace give the way God does: they give people what they *need* rather than what they may *deserve*.

An Indescribable Gift of Grace

Paul closes chapter 9 with a sudden outpouring of gratitude to God for His grace through His Son, Jesus Christ:

> Thanks be to God for His indescribable gift! (v. 15)

One of the best statements on God's grace is found in Romans 5:20:

> The Law came in so that the transgression would increase; but where sin increased, grace abounded all the more.

Wait! Read that verse again! The Law shows us where we have gone wrong, but gives us no power to right that wrong. Grace opens the floodgates of forgiveness instead of burdening us with a load of guilt. Nothing we can do, no need we can face, is beyond the reach of God's grace. He knows that we are completely undeserving, but in His grace, He says, "I'll take care of it. In fact, I took care of it that day on the cross when My only Son died for you."

Amazing grace. Can you encounter it and not respond?

 ## _Living Insights_

Can you remember a time when you were in a tight spot financially, maybe even of your own doing? And then, from a source you least expected, help came?

Maybe it wasn't a money problem. Maybe you were facing a crisis of a different kind, desperate for some other kind of help but seeing no sign of relief. And then help came.

These are examples of the outpouring of God's grace on your life.

Take time to list several specific instances in which you experienced God's amazing grace in your life. Use the space here to write down your memories.

_____

_____

_____

_____

_____

_____

_____

Now examine your response to God's goodness in your life. Perhaps your gratefulness overflowed at the time, but as the months or years have passed, you've begun to take your blessings for granted—to view your possessions as truly your own.

How can you actively remind yourself of God's blessings in your life and respond with thanksgiving?

_____

_____

_____

_____

_____

_____

_____

Does your giving adequately reflect what has been given to you? It's important to plan ahead of time to give graciously and generously to the Lord's work. In what ways might you begin the process of "purposing in your heart" a plan of cheerful giving?

_____

_____

_____

_____

_____

_____

_____

_____

Chapter 5

A BLOODLESS BATTLE
NOBODY NOTICES

2 Corinthians 10:1–6

Do you realize that battles rage around us all the time? School-yard bullies blacken eyes, gangs shoot at each other, nations obliterate other nations. Every day, newspapers and television programs assault us with images of these physical battles. What they don't show, however, is the spiritual battle raging behind the scenes. And that's just fine with the Enemy of our souls, who would prefer that we'd forget this most dangerous battle altogether.

Have you forgotten it? Unfortunately, it's easy to, because the war over our minds and hearts is invisible. Nevertheless, the battlefield is strewn with casualties—those who have been cruelly deceived, brutally assaulted, and fatally misled.

Our Lord wants us to remember this spiritual battle—not to frighten us, but to help us understand it and to empower us to bind up the wounded, release the hostages, and rally those who have retreated.

Satan's Strategy of Deceit

In his letter to the Ephesians, the apostle Paul brought this battle to the forefront of his readers' minds and gave them a strategy for fighting it:

> Finally, be strong in the Lord and in the strength of His might. Put on the full armor of God, so that you will be able to stand firm against the schemes of the devil. (Eph. 6:10–11)

The Greek word for *schemes* is *methodeia*, which means "to act craftily."[1] Satan's deceitful nature is his greatest weapon, more powerful than any on earth, as Paul explained:

> For our struggle is not against flesh and blood, but

---

1. Gerhard Kittel and Gerhard Friedrich, eds., *Theological Dictionary of the New Testament*, translated and abridged in one volume by Geoffrey W. Bromiley (1985; reprint, Grand Rapids, Mich.: William B. Eerdmans Publishing Co., 1992), p. 672.

against the rulers, against the powers, against the world forces of this darkness, against the spiritual forces of wickedness in the heavenly places. (v. 12)

We're not fighting a lone enemy. Satan has an army that's bent on our destruction. Demonic activity is both real and relentless, and we need to be alert, as Peter warns us:

Be of sober spirit, be on the alert. Your adversary, the devil, prowls around like a roaring lion, seeking someone to devour. (1 Pet. 5:8)

Perhaps no modern book illustrates the schemes of Satan better than C. S. Lewis' classic *The Screwtape Letters*. Lewis shines a spotlight on the inner workings of Satan's dark deceptions through fictitious correspondence between an older demon, Screwtape, and his ambitious young nephew, Wormwood:

Doubtless, like all young tempters, you are anxious to be able to report spectacular wickedness. But do remember, the only thing that matters is the extent to which you separate the man from the Enemy. It does not matter how small the sins are, provided that their cumulative effect is to edge the man away from the Light and out into the Nothing. Murder is no better than cards if cards can do the trick. Indeed, the safest road to Hell is the gradual one—the gentle slope, soft underfoot, without sudden turnings, without milestones, without signposts.

Your affectionate uncle
Screwtape[2]

The Believers' Strategic Counterattack

This unseen battle for control of our minds was every bit as real in Paul's day as it is in ours. Let's look first at the skirmish in which the Corinthians were engaged at the time of Paul's letter to them; then we'll study Paul's plan of action.

Conflict Between Paul and the Corinthians

In general, the relationship between Paul and the Corinthians

2. C. S. Lewis, *The Screwtape Letters* (reprint; New York, N.Y.: Macmillan Publishing Co., 1961), p. 56.

was good. There were, however, a few snags. One commentator describes the problems this way:

> In spite of Paul's general satisfaction with the church at Corinth, there was apparently still a group which disputed his apostolic authority, and professed themselves followers of certain leaders whom Paul refers to as "false apostles" ([2 Cor.] 11:13). . . .
> . . . They were Jewish Christians, visitors from outside Corinth (compare 11:4), who came armed with letters of commendation (3:1) claiming for them a higher authority than Paul's (10:7). . . . [Paul] enters into no dispute about their authority or about their teaching, but on the ground of their unchristian behaviour both to the Corinthians (e.g. 11:20) and to himself (compare for example 10:13–15), he feels justified in saying that they are doing the devil's work.[3]

These false apostles were stirring up dissension between the Corinthians and Paul that centered on two issues: Paul's alleged hypocrisy and his supposed fleshly motives. We can infer these complaints from the first two verses of chapter 10:

> Now I, Paul, myself urge you by the meekness and gentleness of Christ—I who am meek when face to face with you, but bold toward you when absent! I ask that when I am present I need not be bold with the confidence with which I propose to be courageous against some, who regard us as if we walked according to the flesh. (2 Cor. 10:1–2)

Don't miss Paul's retort in these verses! The Corinthians apparently accused him of hypocrisy—of being bold in his letters but meek and timid in person. Instead of making an angry defense, he responds in his letter with the very "meekness" they accused him of having in person.

Interestingly, the very meekness and gentleness they despised in Paul were the qualities Jesus used to describe Himself: "I am

---

3. F. F. Bruce, ed., *The International Bible Commentary* (Grand Rapids, Mich.: Zondervan Publishing House, 1986), p. 1406.

gentle and humble in heart" (Matt. 11:29). The false apostles were definitely leading the Corinthians away from Christ and His values, which is why Paul so strongly opposed them with his next words.

Spiritual Warfare Not Fought in the Flesh

Having addressed this first misunderstanding, Paul hones in on the underlying problem, a different kind of conflict—the battle for control of the human mind:

> For though we walk in the flesh, we do not war according to the flesh, for the weapons of our warfare are not of the flesh, but divinely powerful for the destruction of fortresses. We are destroying speculations and every lofty thing raised up against the knowledge of God, and we are taking every thought captive to the obedience of Christ. (2 Cor. 10:3–5)

Paul's imagery is instructive here; he uses a military metaphor, as New Testament scholar Colin G. Kruse notes:

> *Strongholds* [or *fortresses* in the NASB] is an allusion to the towers or raised ramparts used in ancient battles, but here it stands for *arguments and every pretension that sets itself up against the knowledge of God.* It was by the proclamation of the gospel (which involved reasoning and arguing in an effort to remove false barriers thrown up against the truth) that Paul sought to overcome people's resistance and so to *take captive every thought to make it obedient to Christ.* The imagery here is that of a stronghold breached and those sheltering behind its walls taken captive. Paul's purpose is not only to demolish false arguments but also to bring people's thoughts under the lordship of Christ. . . . A passage such as this reminds us that Christian ministry involves a battle for the mind. False arguments need to be demolished, so that people might yield to the truth of the gospel and find life under the lordship of Christ.[4]

---

4. Colin G. Kruse, "2 Corinthians," in *New Bible Commentary: 21st Century Edition*, 4th ed., rev., gen. ed. D. A. Carson, R. T. France, J. A. Motyer, and G. J. Wenham (Downers Grove, Ill.: InterVarsity Press, 1994), p. 1201.

The image of a battleground with its walls and fortresses would have certainly been in Paul's mind as he was writing this passage. The walls around our minds can work for our benefit or our detriment—they can keep out the "good guys" or the "bad guys." Sometimes it's hard for us to tell the difference, isn't it? That's why Paul tells us to take *every* thought captive, to evaluate *every* thought according to Christ's standards and wisdom.

The Issue of Obedience

Lest the Corinthians think he is dodging the issues they've raised, Paul comes back to address the problem they're facing—the conflict within their church that the false prophets have been stirring up. Paul lets them know:

> We are ready to punish all disobedience, whenever your obedience is complete. (v. 6)

In other words, "If I have most of you on my side, we can clean out this whole mess and get on with the business of living victoriously. But first, you're going to have to decide where you stand. You're going to need to take those conflicting thoughts before Christ so He can help you decide." As one commentator explains:

> [Paul's] approach to this particular confrontation in Corinth was twofold. First, it was necessary that the Corinthian church express their subjection to Christ by demonstrating loyalty to His representative Paul (5:20; compare 7:15). In this way their obedience would be complete. Second, when Paul was sure they had repudiated his opponents (compare 6:14–18), he could then deal directly with the false apostles, knowing that the church supported him. He was ready to punish their acts of disobedience to Christ. The word "punish" (*ekdikēsai*) could more forcefully be translated "avenge" (compare 1 Cor. 3:17). In other contexts it describes the wrath of God directed against the enemies of His people (Num. 31:2; Deut. 32:43; Rev. 19:2).[5]

5. David K. Lowery, "2 Corinthians," in *The Bible Knowledge Commentary*, New Testament edition, ed. John F. Walvoord and Roy B. Zuck (Colorado Springs, Colo.: Chariot Victor Publishing, 1983), pp. 576–77.

Some Survival Suggestions

You may not be dealing with false prophets within your church. But whatever your stage of life, whatever your current situation, you can be sure that satanic enemies are trying to scale the walls of your mind. You can also be sure that angels of truth are attempting to get through your fortress as well. How can you tell the difference? What is the most practical way to take all these competing thoughts "captive to the obedience of Christ"? Four words simplify the strategy.

Memorize

If you really want to align your thoughts with Christ's, you first need to know what Christ's thoughts are. You need to absorb His words into your mind and heart, as the psalmist suggested centuries ago:

> Your word I have treasured in my heart,
> That I may not sin against You. (Ps. 119:11)

The verb *treasure* connotes not only an act but an attitude. It means not only placing God's Word in our hearts but also placing a high value on it, as Solomon advised his own son:

> My son, if you will receive my words,
> And treasure my commandments within you,
> Make your ear attentive to wisdom,
> Incline your heart to understanding;
> For if you cry for discernment,
> Lift your voice for understanding;
> If you seek her as silver
> And search for her as for hidden treasures;
> Then you will discern the fear of the Lord,
> And discover the knowledge of God. (Prov. 2:1–5)

There's no more effective way to do that than to memorize sections of God's Word.

Personalize

As you begin to store up God's Word in your heart and mind, it's important to reaffirm that these verses apply to you *personally*. Replace the pronouns in the Scriptures with personal pronouns: *I, me, my, mine*. Let's practice with a passage we studied today:

> For though *I* walk in the flesh, *I* don't war according

to my flesh, for the weapons of my warfare are not of my own flesh, but divinely powerful for the destruction of fortresses. Destroying my speculations and every lofty thing raised up against my knowledge of God, and taking my every thought captive to the obedience of Christ.

Taking the time to personalize Scripture in this way will make the Word of God come alive for you!

Analyze

James 1:23–25 suggests that God's Word is like a mirror to our souls. It doesn't do much good to just catch a glimpse now and then. The only way to make improvements is to stand in front of that mirror and scrutinize what we see. When a passage of Scripture addresses fear, for instance, ask yourself the following questions: *Is there something or someone I am afraid of? How am I handling my fear?*

If it brings to mind an area of your life in which you are weak, ask yourself, *Why am I so vulnerable to this type of temptation? How can I begin to see victory in this area?* In this way, you can remove defensive towers from your life, block by block.

Visualize

How many of us live defeated lives because we can't imagine ourselves living any other way? Immersing ourselves in the Scriptures helps us see that victory is possible, but we must take hold of that vision, believe in it, and accept the help that is available. Listen to these inspirational words of Henry David Thoreau:

> If one advances confidently in the direction of his dreams, and endeavors to live the life which he has imagined, he will meet with a success unexpected in common hours.[6]

The Christian life isn't a contrived public spectacle. It is a deep, spontaneous, abiding, spiritual relationship. One in which, through the invasion of the Scripture and the power of the Holy Spirit, our speculations are overrun, the lofty towers in our minds scaled, and every thought brought captive into obedience to Christ. Then, and

6. Henry David Thoreau, as quoted in *Bartlett's Familiar Quotations*, 14th ed., rev. and enl., ed. Emily Morison Beck (Boston, Mass.: Little, Brown and Co., 1968), p. 683.

only then, will we fully experience the truth. And that truth will make us free (John 8:31–32).

 ## *Living Insights*

Take some time to practice memorizing, personalizing, analyzing, and visualizing a passage of Scripture. See what harmful speculations the Lord will overcome in this exercise. And ask God to show you the areas of your life that need to be fortified by His Word.

Memorize

> How blessed is the man who does not walk in the
>   counsel of the wicked,
> Nor stand in the path of sinners,
> Nor sit in the seat of scoffers!
> But his delight is in the law of the Lord,
> And in His law he meditates day and night.
> He will be like a tree firmly planted by streams
>   of water,
> Which yields its fruit in its season,
> And its leaf does not wither;
> And in whatever he does, he prospers. (Ps. 1:1–3)

Personalize

Rewrite this passage below, adding personal pronouns to help you apply it to your own life.

_____

_____

_____

_____

_____

_____

_____

_____

_____

Analyze

Think about your spiritual life. In which areas do you allow yourself to be influenced by individuals who do not adhere to God's Word? What steps can you take to fill your mind and heart with Scripture? Are you a "tree firmly planted," or do you waver in your commitments?

_____

_____

_____

_____

_____

_____

_____

Visualize

What temptations and evil thoughts are most common in your life? Visualize a situation in which you may be tempted in the future. Describe this situation and how you will respond to it using the techniques you have learned here. What steps will you take to keep God's Word in the forefront of your mind so that you will be able to stand against temptation?

_____

_____

_____

_____

_____

_____

_____

_____

Chapter 6

STABILIZED THOUGH CRITICIZED

2 Corinthians 10:7–18

Success has a spirit-stealing shadow; its name is *Criticism*. Have you noticed it hanging around? It seems to make its discouraging appearance just when we're feeling best about things. After a well-researched presentation to the board; at the end of an inspired lecture to your students; as you complete a project that has demanded your blood, sweat, and tears—that's when it chimes in. "Why didn't you do *this*?" "You forgot about *that*?" "The last person in this position always did it *this* way . . . "

Makes you want to just throw in the towel, doesn't it? But that won't help. A more effective approach is to figure out how to handle criticism when it comes, because it *will* come, no matter how good a job you do. Sometimes it will be constructive and sometimes it will be destructive. But it'll be there, and we all need to be ready for it.

Facts about Criticism We Must Remember

Sometimes criticism comes gently from a sincere heart. But other times it is hurled like a dart by a critic who seems to enjoy pinning others to the wall. Sometimes it is based on knowledge or experience; sometimes it is raised out of ignorance, prejudice, bias, or simply opinion. Whatever its source, a few facts about criticism can ease some of its sting.

First, don't forget that *no one is immune to criticism*. It is an unavoidable part of living among human beings. If you brace yourself for it, you won't feel like the victim of a surprise attack, and you'll be less likely to feel like quitting or fighting back.

Second, remember that *criticism can be taken too lightly or too seriously*. Not all criticism is bad, so take time to listen to it before you decide on your response. If you take it too lightly, you might miss out on some valuable instruction. Criticism can help us see our blind spots, and it can teach us things we may not learn otherwise. If we brush it off, we may fail to grow as we should, and we run the risk of remaining unteachable and immature.

On the other hand, taking criticism too seriously can cause a person to lose heart. It can make us give up on a mission we are fully capable of accomplishing. When we take criticism as absolute truth, we often become intimidated and insecure. When that happens, we risk failing at our current endeavor as well as being afraid to tackle the next one.

The best approach is to take criticism to heart—but take it with a grain of salt! As one man said:

> What people say about us is never quite true; but it is never quite false, either; they always miss the bull's-eye, but they rarely fail to hit the target.[1]

Third, bear in mind that *some criticism needs to be answered, but much of it does not.* Some people are so convinced they're right that they tune out every opposing opinion. They surround themselves with people who never question their decisions and glide through life on a sea of arrogant self-assurance. Others fret over every minute disagreement, apologizing profusely at every complaint, scrambling to please everyone at all times. Obviously, there has to be a balance, but where is it? When should we respond to criticism, and when should we leave it alone?

Start by analyzing the situation. Is the criticism based on a misunderstanding? If so, do your best to clear it up. Is the critic open to dialogue and an exchange of ideas? Hold a meeting of the minds.

But if the critic is a chronic grouch . . . if conversation would only lead to more argument . . . if it is virtually impossible to address the person who originated the criticism . . . let it go. This kind of criticism is not productive, only hurtful. Paying attention to it serves no purpose.

Have you ever noticed how Christ responded to criticism? Sometimes He answered it quickly and directly. But more often, He met His critics with silence—even when they were nailing Him to the cross.

Areas of Criticism Leveled against Paul

Second Corinthians 10 reveals at least three specific criticisms of Paul that had been circulating among the believers at Corinth.

---

1. Sydney Harris, as quoted in *Quote Unquote*, comp. Lloyd Cory (Wheaton, Ill.: Scripture Press Publications, Victor Books, 1977), p. 79.

"Paul, You're a Hypocrite!"

We saw in our last lesson that Paul opens chapter 10 with a tongue-in-cheek response:

> Now I, Paul, myself urge you by the meekness and gentleness of Christ—I who am meek when face to face with you, but bold toward you when absent! (v. 1)

Apparently, rumors had been circulating that Paul was hiding behind his stylus, saying in letters what he didn't have the nerve to say in person.

"Paul, You're Overemphasizing Your Authority!"

On top of this, some people thought he was taking his authority too far. Paul responds with the following:

> For even if I boast somewhat further about our authority, which the Lord gave for building you up and not for destroying you, I will not be put to shame. (v. 8)

Some of the Corinthians resented Paul's leadership, even though it had been given to him by God. Ever been in a similar position? Maybe you've been promoted over former peers at work, or perhaps you've been asked to take over teaching your Bible study group. You've been chosen as a leader, but others may be upset at being passed over. And there might be some who just don't want to follow your leading!

"Paul, You're Unimpressive in Appearance and You're Not That Great to Listen To!"

This one had to sting. Not only was it a low blow, but it was superficial in importance. The Living Bible renders their comments this way:

> "He sounds big, but it's all noise. When he gets here you will see that there is nothing great about him, and you have never heard a worse preacher!" (v. 10)

The critics may have been showing their superficiality with these comments, but of all their complaints, only this one rang true. A second-century Asian presbyter gives this description of Paul:

> [He was] a man small of stature, with a bald head

42

and crooked legs, in a good state of body, with eye-
brows meeting and nose somewhat hooked.[2]

From all accounts, it's doubtful that Paul was handsome. And
he apparently wasn't much to write home about when it came to
public speaking. But never be misled about the vessels in which
God places His riches. Despite his unimpressive appearance, Paul
was used by God to perform an incredible ministry. After all, "God
sees not as man sees, for man looks at the outward appearance, but
the Lord looks at the heart" (1 Sam. 16:7b).

Response to Criticism: Four Thoughtful Answers

People were criticizing Paul's style, his role, and his looks.
Enough to make anyone lose his temper . . . or run and hide! But
the rest of 2 Corinthians 10 shows us how Paul responded—with
calm, reasonable answers.

First, *Paul corrects their perspective.* Gently but firmly, he gets
right to the heart of the problem by telling the Corinthians:

> You are looking at things as they are outwardly. (v. 7a)

Often, when people criticize, it is because they aren't looking
deep enough. They take things at face value, not bothering to look
below the surface or stand in the other person's shoes. This was
true of the Corinthians.

However, a knee-jerk reaction to criticism can cause the same
problem. Before we take offense, we need to take a look at ourselves
from other people's perspective. We may still disagree, but understanding the views of critical people or groups may take some of
the sting out of their statements. It may also take the edge off our
comeback.

Second, *Paul clarifies his motive.* He makes sure his critics understand what's in his heart:

> For even if I boast somewhat further about our au-
> thority, which the Lord gave for building you up and
> not for destroying you, I will not be put to shame,
> for I do not wish to seem as if I would terrify you
> by my letters. (vv. 8–9)

2. As quoted by Richard Longenecker, *The Ministry and Message of Paul* (Grand Rapids,
Mich.: Zondervan Publishing House, 1971), p. 23.

Authority comes with the mandate of building up, not tearing down. It's for the purpose of helping people to their feet, not knocking them to the ground. Although it may include reproof, the reproof is with the purpose of restoration, not condemnation. Paul himself was probably feeling a little kicked around at this time, but instead of lashing out, he gives the Corinthians the benefit of the doubt. He reassures them that he has in no way meant to intimidate them, and he clarifies his motives.

Third, *Paul confesses his authenticity.* He assures the Corinthians that he really is just the way he presents himself, whether in person or in writing:

> Let such a person consider this, that what we are in word by letters when absent, such persons we are also in deed when present.
>
> For we are not bold to class or compare ourselves with some of those who commend themselves; but when they measure themselves by themselves and compare themselves with themselves, they are without understanding. (vv. 11–12)

If you ran into Paul at the grocery store on Thursday, you'd see the same Paul who appeared in the pulpit Sunday morning. He was who he was, and he felt no need to compete with anyone else or hide any part of his personality. He was authentic, through and through.

A word of caution here. Not everyone can make that claim. Many of us spend a great deal of time and effort putting our best foot forward, not realizing that we are undermining the very ministry we are trying to further. Don't try to be something you aren't— even if what you truly are does not seem very holy or impressive. If you're not careful, you will undermine your credibility, and ultimately, your ministry. Authentic human striving and failing is worth far more than phony righteousness.

Fourth, *Paul communicates the facts.* There's nothing like the truth to combat criticism:

> But we will not boast beyond our measure, but within the measure of the sphere which God apportioned to us as a measure, to reach even as far as you. For we are not overextending ourselves, as if we did not reach to you, for we were the first to come even as far as you in the gospel of Christ; not boasting beyond

our measure, that is, in other men's labors, but with the hope that as your faith grows, we will be, within our sphere, enlarged even more by you, so as to preach the gospel even to the regions beyond you. (vv. 13–16a)

Paul may have included this passage as much for his own reassurance as for theirs. He reminds them that his ministry was given to him by God (v. 13) and that his reason for coming to Corinth was to bring them the Good News (v. 14). He also reminds them that he has never lorded his leadership over them; on the contrary, he has looked forward to learning from them (v. 15).

Paul also reiterates that Corinth isn't his only place of ministry; his involvement reaches to "regions beyond" (v. 16a). He separates his ego from the Corinthians' response to him. His world is much bigger than Corinth; he ministers there because God has called him to do so, not because he needs to have a place of power.

Recovering from Criticism: Three Helpful Reminders

It's one thing to read about Paul's response to criticism. It's quite another to keep our cool when our own critics turn up the heat! Let's take a look at what we can do the next time criticism comes our way.

Openly claim your own responsibility. Three of the hardest words in the English language are "You are right." The other three are "I am wrong!" When a critic's words ring true, even just in part, admit it. It will diffuse your anger and help you grow in areas where God may be asking you to change.

Humbly stand where you know you're right. When you've examined yourself, searched the Scriptures, and prayed concerning a critical comment you have received and you still feel that you are in the right, stand firm. Don't let others budge you from what you're sure God has called you to do or to be. Listen to the person's words, but don't feel obligated to confirm them if they aren't true. It's possible to set the criticism aside with humility. As Paul did, "boast in the Lord"—not in yourself.

Calmly allow the Lord to defend you. When you have reached an impasse and you can't convince your critic, rely on the Lord. He knows the truth, and He'll take care of you. Remember verse 18: "For it is not he who commends himself that is approved, but whom the Lord commends."

Living Insights

Do you find yourself more often in the role of criticizer or criticized?

If you are being criticized right now, or if you know that you tend to struggle with how to respond to criticism, this activity is for you. Envision a recent situation in which you faced criticism, and ask yourself the following questions.

Who was doing the criticizing? What were the circumstances?

_____

_____

_____

_____

Was anything happening in that person's life that may have made him or her short-tempered at that time or extra sensitive to the issue at stake?

_____

_____

_____

_____

Was the criticism constructive or destructive? In what ways?

_____

_____

_____

_____

What was the result of the incident? Was it a growth experience? Or did you end up discouraged? Was your relationship with your critic damaged? Did you find out anything about yourself that you did not previously know?

_____

_____

_____

_____

How did you respond to the criticism? What, if anything, might you have done differently, based on what you have learned?

_____

_____

_____

_____

If you find yourself frequently criticizing others, consider the following passages. What does God say about taming the tongue in these verses? Think of some practical ways to apply each passage in your life, and write them below.

Proverbs 12:18

_____

_____

_____

James 3:2–10

_____

_____

_____

Ephesians 4:29

_____

_____

_____

Chapter 7

NOT ALL "MINISTRIES" ARE MINISTRIES

2 Corinthians 11:1–15

D onna was dissatisfied with her job and was suffering through a broken engagement when some friends invited her to a Sunday service at a nearby church commune. She was immediately impressed with the friendly, sincere people she met there and began to attend the services regularly.

She recalls those early days: "Each week you would be welcomed by people who remembered your name, and they would be anxious to tell you of the exciting and wonderful things the group had done that past week. You began to think you were really missing something because you hadn't been a part of the activity."

Within a few months, Donna quit her job and moved into the commune. The next two years were the happiest of her life—she had no responsibilities, no worries. Her life was planned for her by the leaders, and all she had to do was obey, like a child. "They insisted that the answer to life lay in renouncing self and all earthly ties to family, friends, and possessions, and by giving oneself entirely to serving God through the special mission of the commune."

Eventually, though, she began to see the group's dark side. Members were allowed little outside contact—no TV, magazines, newspapers. "You had to turn your mind off," she says. The mysterious female pastor was rarely seen, but members were expected to shower her with expensive gifts, proving their love and devotion.

Donna was repeatedly summoned to bizarre secret meetings in the middle of the night where she and others were publicly humiliated and interrogated, under the guise of destroying their sinful pride. She learned that group members achieved status by informing on the others, so "everybody watched everyone else and cut the other guy's throat in order to save his own neck." For the first time, she also became aware of the complex security system and the ever-present guards she once thought were there for her protection.

It took her three years to escape.[1]

---

1. Story from *The Lure of the Cults and New Religions*, 2d ed., by Ronald Enroth (Downers Grove, Ill.: InterVarsity Press, 1987), pp. 65–74.

48

How did Donna, a Christian college graduate, get sucked into this insidious cult? Jack Sparks, in his fascinating book *The Mindbenders*, explains that cults use three simultaneous methods to lure their members:

> *Step one* is "deprogramming." Your past is all wrong. No matter how sincere your parents or your church may have been, they were wrong. . . . What you always thought was right is wrong, wrong, wrong, wrong, wrong! Reject it. . . .
>
> *Step two* demands your will be captured by the cult. The human will does not functions apart from the mind. Thus, if the normal function of the mind can be altered, control of the will can be gained. Habitual patterns of behavior and response will be broken and a new program put in its place. . . .
>
> *Step three* is the concentrated reprogramming phase. Intensive teaching or indoctrination is the prime means. Day after day, like the dripping of rain, the old concepts are methodically dug up and the old ones planted in their place. A whole new structure is raised. In all of this the convert is hardly aware anything is taking place.[2]

False religions have been around as long as there has been true religion. In Matthew 15:1–14, Jesus confronted the religious leaders of His day for oppressing the Jewish people with their strict laws instead of teaching them to love and obey God.

These religious leaders claimed to know the true way to follow God, but their "ministry" was not really a ministry at all. It was a sham—a distortion of the truth. These leaders were more intent on upholding their own traditions and rules than they were on keeping God's commands. They focused on the fine print of their laws while ignoring God's greater plan. And in the process, they led many other people astray.

Unfortunately, the scribes and Pharisees weren't the only ones to perpetrate this type of fraud. Many religious groups today teach just enough of the truth to sound legitimate, but ultimately they

---

2. Jack Sparks, *The Mindbenders* (Nashville, Tenn.: Thomas Nelson Publishers, 1977), pp. 16–17.

lead their followers away from God, not toward Him. In this study, we'll look first at Jesus' response to the false teachers of His day and then at Paul's warnings to the Corinthians concerning the deception infiltrating their ranks.

Red Flags in Questionable Ministries

Matthew 15:1–14 raises four red flags that signal a questionable ministry.

First: *Questionable ministries substitute human tradition for divine revelation.* The Pharisees had rules for everything, even down to the method for washing hands. In verse 2, we see them trying to undermine Jesus' authority by asking Him this question:

> "Why do Your disciples break the tradition of the elders? For they do not wash their hands when they eat bread."

Jesus answers them with a pointed question of His own:

> "Why do you yourselves transgress the command-ment of God for the sake of your tradition? For God said, 'Honor your father and mother,' and, 'He who speaks evil of father or mother is to be put to death.' But you say, 'Whoever says to his father or mother, "Whatever I have that would help you has been given to God," he is not to honor his father or his mother.' And by this you invalidated the word of God for the sake of your tradition." (vv. 3–6)

Invalidate comes from the Greek prefix *a,* meaning "non," and the root *kuros* or *kurios,* meaning "authority" or "Lord." Jesus was saying that the Pharisees had invalidated God's authority. They had completely ignored God's Word, but were trying to hold the disci-ples accountable to rules made by humans.

When you see any group or leader placing a higher priority on tradition than on God's Word, a warning bell should sound.

Second: *Questionable ministries have externals that seem right, but internally they're far from God.* Jesus follows His question with a sharp rebuke:

> "You hypocrites, rightly did Isaiah prophesy of you:
> 'This people honors Me with their lips,
> But their heart is far away from Me.

50

But in vain do they worship Me,
Teaching as doctrines the precepts of men.'"
(vv. 7–9)

These are strong words. And they point out the fact that questionable ministries quite often sound good, but are internally inconsistent with the Word of God. On the surface, they may appear to honor Him, but under that pious exterior, they are often attempting to gain earthly power, wealth, or status.

Third: *Questionable ministries offer teachings that defile and destroy.*[3] Verses 10–11 wave the next red flag:

After Jesus called the crowd to Him, He said to them, "Hear, and understand. It is not what enters into the mouth that defiles the man, but what proceeds out of the mouth, this defiles the man."

What comes from the mouth originates in the heart (see vv. 19–20). If a person does not have the truth of God in his heart, then the teaching that proceeds from his mouth will reflect that lack of truth. The problem with cults is that their false teaching is not based upon the truth of God's Word. Therefore, it will ultimately bring destruction in the form of spiritual ruin, moral compromise, and emotional instability.

Fourth: *Questionable ministries are led by the spiritually blind.* "Let them alone," Jesus says. "They are blind guides of the blind. And if a blind man guides a blind man, both will fall into a pit" (v. 14). In other words, these spiritually blind leaders are leading their equally blind followers to hell. Jesus warned His disciples—and us—to stay away from them. Don't be enticed by their manipulative schemes.

When you evaluate any religious organization, look for these six "blind spots." Their presence will tell you if the "ministry" is really a ministry.

- *Authoritarianism*—lack of a servant's heart on the part of the leaders; lack of grace

- *Exclusiveness*—the attitude that their way is the only way

- *Greed*—manipulation in order to get money

3. Conversely, orthodox teaching brings glory to God. In the Greek *orthos* means "straight, right" and *doxa* means "glory."

- *Sensuality*—moral impurity, sexual looseness

- *Unaccountability*—secrecy, irresponsibility

- *Rationalization*—defensiveness when confronted, twisting the Scriptures to fit their lifestyle or opinions

The True and the False: Our Need for Discernment

Unfortunately, false teaching continued throughout the first century. Certain misguided leaders were invading the Corinthian church, trying to undermine Paul's authority. So Paul warns the Corinthians about the trap that is being set for them.

The Concern of a Caring Shepherd

In 2 Corinthians 11:1, Paul shows his distaste for what he has to do by asking his readers: "Bear with me in a little foolishness." By *foolishness*, he means having to talk about himself, to boast about his role, to present his credentials. He doesn't like having to do that, but in this case, it's necessary:

> For I am jealous for you with a godly jealousy; for I betrothed you to one husband, so that to Christ I might present you as a pure virgin. But I am afraid that as the serpent deceived Eve by his craftiness, your minds will be led astray from the simplicity and purity of devotion to Christ. (vv. 2–3)

Paul is jealous for the spiritual purity of the Corinthian church, just as a father desires to protect his daughter's sexual purity so that he may present her to her groom. Paul wants to offer Christ a church with an unadulterated loyalty and love for Him.

Differences between the Authentic and the Artificial

In verses 4–12, Paul contrasts the true and the false, showing the Corinthians three ways to know the difference:

> For if one comes and preaches *another* Jesus whom we have not preached, or you receive a *different* spirit which you have not received, or a *different* gospel which you have not accepted, you bear this beautifully. (vv. 4–5, emphasis added)

Difference number one: *False teachers proclaim another Jesus and a different gospel. Another* here means "another of a similar kind." A false teacher may try to copy the truth by mentioning the name of Jesus or throwing in a few points about the Bible, but if his teaching contradicts Scripture in any way, he's fooling you.

Different, on the other hand, means "another of an opposite kind." The false teacher's spirit is opposite of the Spirit of Christ, creating divisiveness. And false teaching opposes the gospel of salvation, usually by adding works. Paul says "you bear this beautifully" with a touch of sarcasm—indicating that the Corinthians were tolerant of the heresy being spread among them.

Difference number two: *False teachers have a lot of charisma.* Many false teachers are hard to resist because they are often extremely talented, persuasive, and influential individuals. In verses 5–6, Paul begins his defense against them:

> For I consider myself not in the least inferior to the most eminent apostles. But even if I am unskilled in speech, yet I am not so in knowledge; in fact, in every way we have made this evident to you in all things.

Basically, Paul's argument is this: "I'm just as authentic as the original twelve apostles. Place me next to Peter, Andrew, James, or John, and I can measure up with the best of them. Others may be more eloquent, but what I lack in eloquence, I more than compensate for in knowledge, for God has taught me what I'm teaching you." The Corinthians were getting carried away by the persuasive delivery of the false teachers, but Paul reminds them to check the content against what they know to be true.

Difference number three: *False teachers are greedy.* Some of these teachers were telling the Corinthians that Paul's words weren't worth hearing because he didn't charge an admission fee. Paul addresses this accusation in verses 7–9:

> Or did I commit a sin in humbling myself so that you might be exalted, because I preached the gospel of God to you without charge? I robbed other churches, taking wages from them to serve you; and when I was present with you and was in need, I was not a burden to anyone; for when the brethren came from Macedonia, they fully supplied my need, and in everything I kept myself from being a burden to you, and will continue to do so.

Paul had received offerings from other churches so that he could remain financially free in wealthy Corinth; he never wanted it said that he came to them for the money they could have amply provided.[4]

Paul concludes his personal defense in verses 10–12:

> As the truth of Christ is in me, this boasting of mine will not be stopped in the regions of Achaia. Why? Because I do not love you? God knows I do!
>
> But what I am doing, I will continue to do, so that I may cut off opportunity from those who desire an opportunity to be regarded just as we are in the matter about which they are boasting.

Because of his love for the Corinthians, Paul says that he will continue to point out these wolves in sheep's clothing (see Matt. 7:15; Acts 20:29).

The Reason Behind the Lure of False "Ministries"

Paul may have been upset by the popularity of the false teachers in Corinth, but he wasn't surprised. He knew where they came from:

> For such men are false apostles, deceitful workers, disguising themselves as apostles of Christ. No wonder, for even Satan disguises himself as an angel of light. Therefore it is not surprising if his servants also disguise themselves as servants of righteousness. (2 Cor. 11:13–15a)

Satan—the archenemy of Christ—is behind every false teacher. He disguises himself and his followers as something good and right, but their "end will be according to their deeds" (v. 15b). They'll fall victim to their own lies and will perish without Christ.

To Keep from Falling for the Phony . . .

Here are two suggestions to help you discern authentic ministries from artificial ones.

First: *Probe into the doctrinal statement of the organization.* Does it proclaim the deity of Jesus Christ as the eternal Son of God and second member of the Trinity? And does it offer salvation as the

---

4. A warning against greed in ministry appears in 1 Peter 5:1–4: "Shepherd of the flock of God . . . not for sordid gain, but with eagerness" (v. 2).

free gift of God, purchased by Christ on the cross and available only through grace, not works? Does it uphold belief in Christ's death and bodily resurrection? These are the basic tenets of the Christian faith; if anything is missing, it's heresy. Leave it alone.

Second: *Examine the private lives of leadership.* Are the leaders accountable to anyone? Do they have servant's hearts, or do they seem to have a desire for others to serve them? Are they free from sexual and moral impurity? Free of greed and financial impropriety? Willing to answer hard questions openly and honestly? If not, back away.

Remember, you have a message of hope based on Jesus Christ and the Bible. When you come into contact with a cult member, share that message. Stay on the offensive: know your Bible, stick to the issues of Christ and salvation, and pray that this person will respond. But don't entertain his or her doctrine—not even for a minute!

 Living Insights

FBI agents are trained to recognize counterfeit money by becoming so intensely familiar with real currency that a fraud is immediately recognizable. By the same token, we must be knowledgeable about our faith in God so that we will not be led astray by false teaching.

How familiar are you with the basic tenets of the Christian faith? What would you say that the essentials of the faith are? Are there areas about which you would like to know more? What are they?

_____

_____

_____

_____

_____

What kinds of cults are you aware of in your community? How do you respond when you encounter their members or their message?

_____

_____

_____

_____

_____

There may be cults of which you are not aware. Perhaps even some organizations that you have assumed to be Christian are really not. Which ministries do you currently support financially?

_____

_____

_____

How much do you really know about their beliefs? How could you find out more?

_____

_____

_____

Are your children or friends involved in any groups that claim to be Christian? Have you taken the time to check them out and be sure they are legitimate? How might you go about doing so?

_____

_____

_____

_____

These questions may have raised some issues that you would like to study further, so take time to explore your areas of interest. Make sure you are firmly rooted in the basics of your faith.

Some helpful resources on theology and the Christian life are: *Basic Christianity* by John Stott; *Knowing God* by. J. I. Packer; *Living by the Book* by Howard Hendricks; *A Survey of Bible Doctrine* by Charles Ryrie; *Know What You Believe* by Paul Little; *Essential Christianity: A Handbook of Basic Christian Doctrines* by Walter Martin; and *Understanding Doctrine: What It Is and Why It Matters* by Alister McGrath.

Chapter 8

THE FLIP SIDE OF "FANTASTIC"

2 Corinthians 11:16–33

Be honest. When asked how you're doing, have you ever tossed off a glib "Fine!," "Great!," or "Wonderful!"—even if it isn't the truth?

Of course you have—we all have! Maybe it's just a habit, or maybe we feel that it's just not the right moment for a more honest response. Maybe it's pride or a desire to spare others the pain and disillusionment we're really feeling. Or maybe we're just trying the best we can to maintain our faith in the face of disheartening circumstances.

Whatever the reason, every time we slap on a smile to hide our true feelings, we create a false impression. Not just of our own lives, but of the Christian life in general. And there's no reason to fake it, because in reality, life is *not* just a bowl of cherries. And we don't always feel fantastic!

A Good Response to "How Ya Doin'?"

So if we can't say, "Great!" but it's also not always appropriate to unload all the details, how can we respond when someone asks how we're doing? Tucked away in Romans 5 is the brief outline of a proper response.

> Therefore, having been justified by faith, we have
> peace with God through our Lord Jesus Christ. (v. 1)

Although life may seem less than fantastic at times, there is one thing that remains true for the believer: *we have peace with God.* That's the first part of our answer. The second part comes from the next verse:

> Through whom also we have obtained our introduc-
> tion by faith into this grace in which we stand; and
> we exult in hope of the glory of God. (v. 2)

Not only do we have peace with God, but *we have the hope of the glory of God.* We know that no matter what happens, God will be glorified in our lives—and eventually, we will share in His glory. As a result, we can "exult" even in the midst of difficult circumstances.

> And not only this, but we also exult in our tribulations, knowing that tribulation brings about perseverance; and perseverance, proven character; and proven character, hope; and hope does not disappoint, because the love of God has been poured out within our hearts through the Holy Spirit who was given to us. (vv. 3–5)

The third part of our answer is this: *we are inundated with the love of God.*

The man who wrote these letters was intimately acquainted with the less-than-fantastic side of life. As we return to 2 Corinthians, we'll see some of the details of his difficulties.

An Honest Reaction to "What about Them?"

In Paul's second letter to the Corinthians, we get a realistic view of an obedient servant of God who is not experiencing life at its most pleasant. In fact, he is *very concerned.*

When Paul left the Corinthians, the church was strong and healthy. His absence, however, created a vacuum, and false teachers rushed in to fill it. They looked better than Paul, preached better than Paul, and they had more impressive credentials. And soon many of the Corinthians had switched loyalties. So Paul was forced into doing something he hated to do—boast about himself (11:1–6). In verses 16–33, he reasserts his credentials. He apologizes for doing so in 16–19, but verse 20 shows us why it was necessary:

> For you tolerate it if anyone enslaves you, anyone devours you, anyone takes advantage of you, anyone exalts himself, anyone hits you in the face.

Paul was concerned about the Corinthians. Not only were they being misled, but they were also being mistreated. The Corinthians lacked the discernment to see through these false teachers.

How could the Corinthians have been so deceived? The false teachers in Paul's day were not obvious. They looked and sounded like believers; that's how they were able to sway so many members of the church. And it's important to remember that today's false teachers are no different. They may be wolves in sheep's clothing, but to the undiscerning eye, they sure do look a lot like sheep!

Compared to these false teachers, Paul knew he came up short in the charisma department. His credentials, however, were more sound. The false teachers had pulled rank on Paul in several areas, and it was time for him to stand up for himself.

> To my shame I must say that we have been weak by comparison.
>
> But in whatever respect anyone else is bold—I speak in foolishness—I am just as bold myself. Are they Hebrews? So am I. Are they Israelites? So am I. Are they descendants of Abraham? So am I. Are they servants of Christ? I speak as if insane—I more so. (vv. 21–23a)

These imposters had résumés that looked pretty impressive. But they had none of the credentials that count in the eyes of God. They did not understand the truth of God's Word, and there is no evidence that they had sincere hearts and a true love for God.

Paul continues with a series of proofs for his servanthood. But there isn't a grand achievement listed among them. Instead, he delineates his defeats. He lists his disappointments, pressures, pains, weaknesses, needs, and hurts—essentially, he describes life on the flip side of fantastic.

Odd, isn't it? Especially for someone who is trying to win back his church from some pretty charismatic characters! But Paul wasn't trying to impress; he was trying to illustrate. He was showing them a picture of a true servant of Christ so they would recognize the poor imitations in their midst.

A Realistic Portrayal of "What It's Like"

Allow Paul's next words to sink into your soul:

> In far more labors, in far more imprisonments, beaten times without number, often in danger of death. Five times I received from the Jews thirty-nine lashes. Three times I was beaten with rods, once I was stoned, three times I was shipwrecked, a night and a day I have spent in the deep. I have been on frequent journeys, in dangers from rivers, dangers from robbers, dangers from my countrymen, dangers from

the Gentiles, dangers in the city, dangers in the wilderness, dangers on the sea, dangers among false brethren; I have been in labor and hardship, through many sleepless nights, in hunger and thirst, often without food, in cold and exposure. (vv. 23b–27)

Are you picturing these circumstances in your mind? With these words, Paul establishes the fact, once and for all, that the Christian life is not always "fantastic." It may involve tremendous suffering at times. But the true servant of God is willing to undergo whatever is necessary for the sake of the Gospel. And Paul wasn't the only one to walk this painful path (see Heb. 12:2–3; 1 Pet. 2:21; Heb. 11:35–38).

As if the physical suffering weren't enough, Paul often ached with anxiety, just like many of us:

Apart from such external things, there is the daily pressure on me of concern for all the churches. (2 Cor. 11:28)

Far from claiming any glory for these things, Paul is humble:

Who is weak without my being weak? Who is led into sin without my intense concern? (v. 29)

Unlike the false teachers who were lording their leadership over the Corinthians, Paul puts himself right on their level. When you've struggled, you don't condemn those who struggle—you empathize. When you've been weakened, you understand someone who is in a time of weakness. When you've suffered like Paul, your faith moves out of the realm of the theoretical and into the arena of the practical. It becomes *real*.

Earlier in the chapter, Paul listed his credentials. In the next few verses, he shows us the credentials that really count—and as he does so, he paints a portrait of himself most of us would be embarrassed to hang on the wall:

If I have to boast, I will boast of what pertains to my weakness. The God and Father of the Lord Jesus, He who is blessed forever, knows that I am not lying. In Damascus the ethnarch under Aretas the king was guarding the city of the Damascenes in order to seize me, and I was let down in a basket through a window in the wall, and so escaped his hands. (vv. 30–33)

There's nothing very impressive about being dumped in a basket and let down through a window to flee for your life! Paul never received royal treatment for serving Christ. But that wasn't what he was looking for.

Three things stand out about this great man of God. First, *he doesn't deny the pain and pressures of life*. Never once does he suggest that following Christ is a guaranteed formula for a perfect, fantastic, problem-free life.

Second, *he doesn't market his misery*. It had to be forced out of him. You even get the impression he has difficulty talking about himself in these terms.

Third, *he doesn't explain why*. Verse 33 ends abruptly. Paul makes no attempt to analyze or moralize. He doesn't give a treatise on why Christians suffer. He just leaves us with the image of a man who is weak and helpless being dropped in a basket and fleeing for his life. Why? Perhaps because we don't always find out the reasons for our suffering while we're on this earth. Perhaps because Paul wants to leave his readers with a picture, not of a great man who has it all together, but of a humble man who knows what life is like—but still offers hope.

A Humble Answer to "Who Am I?"

One of the greatest questions we can ever answer is, "How ya doin'?" Because an honest response also answers the question, "Who am I?"

The truth is that, like Paul, we are weak. We are sinful. We are helpless and in need of others. And most of all, we are in need of God.

 Living Insights

Eugene Peterson has written an insightful book called *Five Smooth Stones for Pastoral Work*. In it, he addresses the topic of suffering in a way likely to spark some new thoughts in your mind. Take a moment to read this excerpt:

> Nothing contrasts pastoral work and the humanist traditions more clearly than their respective responses

to suffering. The modern humanist traditions see suffering as a deficiency—usually under the analogy of sickness. Something has gone wrong, and a therapist is called in to set it right. . . .

. . . Pastoral work joins the sufferer. . . .

The pastor who accepts this work will neither attempt explanations of suffering nor mount programs for the elimination of it. . . .

Pastors have no business interfering with another's sorrow, or manipulating it. Suffering is an event in which we are particularly vulnerable to grace, able to recognize dimensions in God and depths in the self. . . .

In the process we will learn that ruins are not disasters: we no longer panic in the face of ruin. One cannot hurry healing. Suffering . . . is not an ominous disaster to be avoided but a difficult, healing operation to be accepted.[1]

How do you normally respond to a friend who is suffering? What is your first inclination?

_____

_____

_____

_____

_____

_____

How do you usually respond to the first signs of suffering edging its way into your own life? What is your response as time goes on?

_____

_____

1. Eugene H. Peterson, *Five Smooth Stones for Pastoral Work* (Atlanta, Ga.: John Knox Press, 1980), pp. 111, 110, 112, 118

_____

_____

_____

_____

_____

Think back over what you have read today, both in Paul's letter and in the excerpt from Eugene Peterson's book. Has anything changed in the way you view suffering? Are there any thoughts you would like to explore further?

_____

_____

_____

_____

_____

_____

_____

Chapter 9

GLOVES OF GRACE FOR HANDLING THORNS

2 Corinthians 12:1–10

Ever met one of those people who seems to have it all together? Someone who has the looks, the brains, the talent, the spirit, and the personality, all rolled into one?

Deep down, we know that everyone has feelings of inadequacy. But when we encounter people who are incredibly intelligent and magnificently gifted, it's hard to imagine that they ever feel the way we do. When we encounter a person who is deeply committed to the Lord and well versed in the Scriptures, we find it difficult to believe that he or she could ever lack confidence.

Intelligence, giftedness, and spiritual depth are all blessings from God, to be used for His purposes. No matter how great our abilities, regardless of how well honed our skills, every good thing about us is a gift from the Father. The problem is that we face a daily temptation to glory in our own accomplishments. But in 1 Corinthians 4:7, Paul reminds us of the way things really are:

> For who regards you as superior? What do you have
> that you did not receive? And if you did receive it,
> why do you boast as if you had not received it?

Everything we have, we owe to God. It's God's strength, not our own, that makes us adequate for any situation. And He has a way of gently reminding us of that fact! To keep us from relying on our own strength to make it through life, God may choose to give us a thorn in the flesh, just like He gave Paul. Let's look at 2 Corinthians 12 to gain more insight into this significant truth.

A Classic Example: Paul

It's hard to be any more "adequate" than Paul was. Well educated, well grounded in Scripture, dedicated to God, and with a far-reaching ministry, he was and still is one of the greats of the Christian faith. As we've read before, however, the Corinthians needed to be reminded why they should follow his teachings. Paul reiterates his résumé in chapter 11. Then, at the beginning of chapter 12, he explains himself:

> Boasting is necessary, though it is not profitable. (v. 1a)

It's helpful to think of this statement in terms of horizontal and vertical meaning. Horizontally—among people—it is sometimes necessary to display our credentials. There are times when people may need to see our résumés. But vertically—before God—it is never valuable. In fact, it is downright laughable. Can you imagine the Creator of the universe being impressed by our pitiful list of accomplishments? He knows all about them anyway.

At this point in history, it was necessary for Paul to show his résumé to the Corinthians, even though they'd seen it before. But this time, he reveals something that he's never mentioned before, an event that is not recounted anywhere else in the Scriptures.

A Man of Unsurpassed Spiritual Ecstasy

Paul writes of this experience in the third person, but scholars agree that he is actually describing something that happened to himself (see also verse 7, noting the personal pronouns). He may have chosen to write this way out of modesty, not wanting to suggest that he was a special kind of Christian.[1] The timing of the event places it during Paul's wilderness experience just after his conversion, a time when he was not in contact with anyone. He writes:

> But I will go on to visions and revelations of the Lord. I know a man in Christ who fourteen years ago—whether in the body I do not know, or out of the body I do not know, God knows—such a man was caught up to the third heaven.[2] And I know how such a man—whether in the body or apart from the body I do not know, God knows—was caught up

1. See Murray J. Harris, "2 Corinthians," in *The Expositor's Bible Commentary*, gen. ed. Frank E. Gaebelein (Grand Rapids, Mich.: Zondervan Publishing House, Regency Reference Library, 1976), vol. 10, p. 395.

2. "The third heaven designates a place beyond the immediate heaven of the earth's atmosphere and beyond the further heaven of outer space and its constellations into the presence of God himself." Philip Edgecumbe Hughes, note on 2 Corinthians 12:2–4, in *The NIV Study Bible*, gen. ed. Kenneth L. Barker (Grand Rapids, Mich.: Zondervan Bible Publishers, 1985), p. 1776.

into Paradise, and heard inexpressible words, which
a man is not permitted to speak. (vv. 1b–4)

Apparently, Paul had been in the literal presence of God
Himself—but for fourteen years he had kept it to himself. Even at
this writing he seems reluctant to let people know of it, bringing
it up only in hopes of persuading the Corinthians that his teachings
are genuinely inspired by God.

A Man of Uncommon Authenticity

Most people who have had unusual experiences are ready to
sign book deals before the ink is dry in their journals. Paul, though,
gives only the sketchiest details, and even then, he couches them
in modesty:

On behalf of such a man I will boast; but on my
own behalf I will not boast, except in regard to my
weaknesses. For if I do wish to boast I will not be
foolish, for I will be speaking the truth; but I refrain
from this, so that no one will credit me with more
than he sees in me or hears from me. (vv. 5–6)

Paul adamantly wanted his readers to understand that he is
nothing more than what they've known him to be. Just a sincere,
devoted man of God, with flaws and weaknesses like theirs.

Still, an experience like that could go to anyone's head, even
Paul's. So God gave him a constant reminder of his humanness, his
inadequacy, his utter need to rely on God.

A Man of Inescapable Pain

Verses 7 and 8 open a window into Paul's private pain:

Because of the surpassing greatness of the revelations,
for this reason, to keep me from exalting myself, there
was given me a thorn in the flesh, a messenger of
Satan to torment me—to keep me from exalting
myself! Concerning this I implored the Lord three
times that it might leave from me. (vv. 7–8)

Theologians have speculated on what the "thorn" symbolizes,
although Paul wasn't specific. Calvin suggested that it represents
spiritual temptations—the urge for Paul to doubt and waver in his
faith when things got hard. Martin Luther thought it referred to

temptations and persecutions. Some believe it was sexual temptation, since Paul was celibate. Others have guessed disfigurement or disease such as epilepsy, malarial fevers, or severe headaches. Some speculate that it was a speech impediment. The most common theory is that it was failing eyesight, in light of his comment in his letter to the Galatians:

> See with what large letters I am writing to you
> with my own hand. (6:11)

Earlier in that same letter, Paul remarks that at one time, the Galatians' feelings of friendship for him had been so deep that "if possible, you would have plucked out your eyes and given them to me" (4:15). This seems to strengthen the argument that Paul's eyes were weak. The words Paul used also indicate that his weakness was more than just inconvenient; it must have been painful as well. As one author notes, concerning the word *thorn:*

> We have the idea of something sharp and painful
> sticking deeply in the flesh so that it remains there
> and cannot be drawn out. . . . [The verb in this
> passage is rare and is translated as *torment.*] Derived
> from the word for *knuckles,* it means "to strike with
> the fist so that the hard knuckles make a blow that
> sting and crush the opponent."[3]

Whatever the nature of the "thorn" that was tormenting Paul, it was severe enough for him to plead with the Lord to take it away. But the thorn served a purpose, and God allowed it to remain.

A Man of Paradoxical Power

God said no to Paul's request, but He explained His response:

> And He has said to me, "My grace is sufficient for
> you, for power is perfected in weakness." (2 Cor. 12:9a)

The Greek term for *perfected* means "complete." It is the same word Jesus cried out as He hung on the cross: *"Tetelestai!"*—"It is finished!" The reason the pain couldn't be removed is that it created in Paul a necessary incompleteness and a dependency on God. God

---

3. R. C. H. Lenski, *The Interpretation of St. Paul's First and Second Epistles to the Corinthians* (1937; reprint, Minneapolis, Minn.: Augsburg Publishing House, 1963), p. 1300.

used Paul's weakness to demonstrate His own grace and sufficiency despite the circumstances. He completed the picture.

Once Paul understood, He stopped asking for this weakness to be removed:

> Most gladly, therefore, I will rather boast about my weaknesses, so that the power of Christ may dwell in me. Therefore I am well content with weaknesses, with insults, with distresses, with persecutions, with difficulties, for Christ's sake; for when I am weak, then I am strong. (vv. 9b–10)

When Thorns Pierce Your Adequacy

No doubt you, like Paul, can think of at least one failure or difficulty in your life that makes you feel inadequate at times. Maybe it's time to stop bemoaning it and accept it as a gift. When you come across thorns in your own life, here are some hints for handling them with gloves of grace.

First, *look within*. Does this weakness affect your pride? Does it hinder your progress in any area or cause you to have to work harder to accomplish your goals? It may be God's avenue of grace in your life—the chance for you to see His power at work.

Second, *look beyond*. Instead of focusing on what you can't do because of your inability, look at what that inability can lead to: a greater dependence on God.

 Living Insights

Perhaps one reason Paul didn't specify the nature of his "thorn" was so that we wouldn't limit its application to our lives. It really doesn't matter much whether it was a disability or a blow to his pride or an area of continual temptation. The point is that God allows inadequacy in our lives for two reasons: so that we will rely on Him, and so that His power will have an avenue through which to flow.

Is there something in your life that continually trips you up or holds you back? Describe the ways this "thorn" affects your life and ministry to others.

_____

_____

_____

_____

_____

Have you ever considered viewing this weakness as a friend? Try to do so now. In what ways have you already benefited spiritually as a result of its presence in your life?

_____

_____

_____

_____

_____

If you can't think of any spiritual benefits you've experienced so far, what do you think has hindered you?

_____

_____

_____

_____

_____

Read 2 Cor. 12:9. Write it below.

_____

_____

_____

_____

_____

_____

God's grace is sufficient to meet all our needs! His power is revealed through our weaknesses. That's a promise we can take to heart!

Chapter 10
HONESTY WRAPPED IN HUMILITY
2 Corinthians 12:7–18

Have you ever reached out to pick a rose, only to feel the sharp prick of a thorn?

Of course, if given the choice, we would all prefer life to be a bed of roses rather than a tangle of thorns. But often God works through our most painful circumstances to teach us lessons about our dependence on Him. Even when we don't want to cooperate. Even when we resent or resist Him. Even when we forget He's there. It's no secret:

> God causes all things to work together for good to those who love God, to those who are called according to His purpose. For those whom He foreknew, He also predestined to become conformed to the image of His Son. (Rom. 8:28–29a)

We can count on it: God will conform His children to the image of His Son—or, as J. B. Phillips puts it, to the "family likeness of His Son."[1] And how will He do this? By continually teaching, changing, and developing us. With God, no day is ever wasted. No disappointment is outside His appointment. No test is ever superfluous. No surprise to us ever catches Him off guard. He never gets off course, never forgets the game plan, never contradicts His overall purpose for us. God reminded Jeremiah of this great truth:

> "For I know the plans that I have for you," declares the Lord, "plans for welfare and not for calamity to give you a future and a hope." (Jer. 29:11)

Paul also reminds us of one of God's greatest promises in the first chapter of the book of Philippians:

> He who began a good work in you will perfect it until the day of Christ Jesus. (v. 6b)

---

1. J. B. Phillips, *The New Testament in Modern English*, rev. ed. (New York, N.Y.: Macmillan Publishing Co., 1972), p. 324.

Some Methods God Employs to Teach His Children

God uses many things to shape us into Christlikeness. Here are a few; no doubt you can add several more.

- By meeting our needs when we are helpless, He teaches us *trust*.

- By making us wait for what we need or want, He teaches us *patience*.

- By stretching us beyond the realm of the familiar, He teaches us *vision*.

- By taking us through the consequences of wrong choices, He teaches us *values*.

- By allowing us to fail and make mistakes, He teaches us *wisdom*.

- By permitting pain and affliction, He teaches us *humility*.

- By involving us in the lives of difficult people, He teaches us *unselfishness*.

Do you see the one characteristic every item on that list has in common? They're all unpleasant or uncomfortable. If life were easy, we'd never bother to change. Just as the pain of a toothache prompts us to visit the dentist, the difficulty of life sends us on our knees before the Father—and provides the motivation for us to change our ways.

Paul was no stranger to this concept. Let's examine how God used two things from this list—pain and relationships—to mold Paul into Christ's image.

The Vertical Message of Pain: Humility

We began studying 2 Corinthians 12 in the last chapter. Now let's pick up where we left off—in the middle of a discussion about pain. We'll begin with verse 7, where Paul discusses his "thorn in the flesh" and the reason why it was given to him.

> Because of the surpassing greatness of the revelations, for this reason, to keep me from exalting myself, there was given me a thorn in the flesh, a messenger of Satan to torment me—to keep me from exalting myself!

We tend to think that God should remove things like chronic

71

pain from those who serve Him so that they won't be hindered in their ministry. But in Paul, God saw something that could hinder his ministry far more than a disability—He saw the potential for spiritual conceit.

In verse 8, we learn that Paul prayed three times for this "thorn" to be removed. He indicates that God never took it away. And it seems that he never made the request again. But he never stops talking about the benefits he received by having this thorn:

> [The Lord] has said to me, "My grace is sufficient for you, for power is perfected in weakness." Most gladly, therefore, I will rather boast about my weaknesses so that the power of Christ may dwell in me. Therefore I am well content with weaknesses, with insults, with distresses, with persecutions, with difficulties, for Christ's sake; for when I am weak, then I am strong. (vv. 9–10)

That thorn, whatever it was, allowed God's power to be on display. It kept Paul humble, and it kept him on his knees. No doubt he would give a hearty "amen" to these words of an unknown Confederate soldier:

> I asked God for strength that I might achieve.
> I was made weak that I might learn humbly to obey.
>
> I asked God for health that I might do greater things.
> I was given infirmity that I might do better things.
>
> I asked for riches that I might be happy.
> I was given poverty that I might be wise.
>
> I asked for power that I might have the praise of men.
> I was given weakness that I might feel the need of
>   God.
>
> I asked for all things that I might enjoy life.
> I was given life that I might enjoy all things.
>
> I got nothing that I asked for
> but everything I had hoped for . . .
>
> Almost despite myself my unspoken prayers were
>   answered.

I am among all men most richly blessed.[2]

The Horizontal Test of Relationships: Unselfishness

God doesn't use only pain to help us learn; He also uses people. In verses 11–18, Paul returns to the subject of his relationship with the Corinthians. As we learned earlier, false teachers in Corinth had attacked Paul's reputation. And the Corinthians, supposedly Paul's friends, had responded by either keeping quiet or by agreeing! Since they haven't defended him, he's driven to defend himself with what he calls "foolish boasting."

> I have become foolish; you yourselves compelled me. Actually I should have been commended by you, for in no respect was I inferior to the most eminent apostles, even though I am a nobody. The signs of a true apostle were performed among you with all perseverance, by signs and wonders and miracles. For in what respect were you treated as inferior to the rest of the churches, except that I myself did not become a burden to you? Forgive me this wrong! (vv. 11–13)

With tongue in cheek, Paul reminds them that he had every right to expect the Corinthians to provide his living expenses for preaching the Gospel. After all, he worked there long enough for the church to become established and for offerings to be taken to help support his ministry.

Paul served the Corinthian believers tirelessly without pay, even though there would have been nothing wrong with asking to be paid. Instead, he worked two jobs. He had a paying job as a tentmaker and also pastored the church at Corinth, relying on gifts from other churches to make ends meet.

Have you ever had a trusted friend take advantage of you? Talk about you behind your back? Rip you off in some way? Then you can imagine how Paul felt. But despite the Corinthians' disloyalty, he next says that he wants to come and visit them (v. 14). Why on earth would he want to do that?

There are several general reasons, and they're woven into the rest of this passage. The main reason is that Paul was not a man of

2. By an unknown Confederate soldier, as quoted in Tim Hansel's *When I Relax I Feel Guilty* (Elgin, Ill.: David C. Cook Publishing Co., 1979), p. 89.

pride; the thorn had taken care of that. His feelings may have been hurt, but his ego didn't stand in the way of his mission. Beyond that, however, he had five specific reasons for wanting to continue his relationship with the Corinthians—and all five highlight his humility.

First, *he had no image to protect.* In verse 11, he said, "I am a nobody." This wasn't false humility; remember, he had been to the "third heaven." He had been in the presence of God. If that won't put you in your place, nothing will! He didn't care how anyone viewed him. He only cared how they viewed God.

Second, *he didn't keep score.* He didn't care who owed whom what. He didn't keep track of who had invited him over for dinner or whose turn it was to wash the communion dishes. He mentioned the salary issue only to make a point, as we see in verse 14:

> Here for this third time I am ready to come to you, and I will not be a burden to you; for I do not seek what is yours, but you; for children are not responsible to save up for their parents, but parents for their children.

Far from trying to collect on old debts, he still plans to pay his own way on his upcoming visit. He's interested in the people of Corinth themselves, not in what he might get from them.

Third, *he had a servant's heart.* In verse 15, he takes the idea a step further:

> I will most gladly spend and be expended for your souls. If I love you the more, am I to be loved less?

Like Jesus Himself, Paul did not want to go to the Corinthians to be served, but to serve (see Matt. 20:28).

Fourth, *he refused to take advantage of them.* With a touch of humor, Paul reminds them of his commitment to them:

> But be that as it may, I did not burden you myself; nevertheless, crafty fellow that I am, I took you in by deceit. Certainly I have not taken advantage of you through any of those whom I have sent to you, have I? I urged Titus to go, and I sent the brother with him. Titus did not take any advantage of you, did he? (2 Cor. 12:16–18a)

He isn't afraid to come back to them because he knows his slate is clean.

Fifth, *he modeled what he expected of others.* Look how he concludes verse 18:

> Did we not conduct ourselves in the same spirit and
> walk in the same steps?

The next time you feel offended or mistreated by someone, ask yourself these questions: Is my image a little too important to me? Do I tend to keep score? Is my goal to serve or to be served? Have I taken advantage of this person? Am I modeling what I'm expecting from others?

Ways We Can Accelerate the Learning Process

Let's face it—we're going to experience pain. It might be physical, it might be relational, but it's going to come. When it does, how can we learn from it?

First, *instead of reacting to pain as an enemy, remain teachable.* Sometimes we live as though the Bible says we are supposed to "feel happy" every day of our lives. But it doesn't. There's a difference between "feeling happy" and having joy even in difficult circumstances. So when pain comes along, instead of treating it as an enemy, learn to see it as a friend. Instead of asking God to take it away, ask Him what He wants you to learn from it.

Second, *rather than resenting everyone because of a few who've offended you, stay involved.* It's through difficult people that we learn unselfishness. And besides, we can't be a witness on a deserted island! We need to continue to minister to people, even when we have been wronged.

Third, *in place of becoming offended and resentful, trust God.* When you realize He is trying to conform you into the image of His Son, your difficult experiences will take on new meaning. Trust Him . . . even when He doesn't explain why. He will honor that response. After all, He loves you!

 Living Insights

Are you currently experiencing painful situations? Are they spiritual, emotional, relational or physical? Use the space on the next page to describe what you're going through.

_____

_____

_____

_____

_____

What has been the main theme of your prayers regarding this situation? What has been God's response?

_____

_____

_____

_____

_____

In light of what you've studied here, do you think your prayers are in line with His purposes? Why or why not?

_____

_____

_____

What qualities do you think God might be trying to help you develop at this time? Do you think you are cooperating with this process or resisting it?

_____

_____

_____

_____

In what ways might you better align your goals with God's?

_____

_____

_____

Chapter 11

THREADS FOR MENDING
FRAYED FEELINGS
2 Corinthians 12:19–13:4

I t's been said that Christians are a lot like porcupines. We have a lot of good points, but it's hard to get close to us! Unfortunately, our prickly personalities and strong opinions often cause conflicts and hurt feelings within the body of Christ.

Sometimes it seems we can't agree about anything. Not only do we have denominational differences, but we have so many splinter groups that even the splinters have splinters! And even when we find a group we agree with, we may have conflicts with people within it.

This pattern of disunity is a far cry from what God had in mind for His church. In fact, His strongest words are often used in the context of relationships. Romans 12 gives some practical advice on how to relax our quills so we can huddle closer without hurting each other:

> Be devoted to one another in brotherly love; give preference to one another in honor; not lagging behind in diligence, fervent in spirit, serving the Lord; rejoicing in hope, persevering in tribulation, devoted to prayer, contributing to the needs of the saints, practicing hospitality.
>
> Bless those who persecute you; bless and do not curse. Rejoice with those who rejoice, and weep with those who weep. Be of the same mind toward one another; do not be haughty in mind, but associate with the lowly. Do not be wise in your own estimation. Never pay back evil for evil to anyone. Respect what is right in the sight of all men. If possible, so far as it depends on you, be at peace with all men. Never take your own revenge, beloved, but leave room for the wrath of God, for it is written, "Vengeance is Mine, I will repay," says the Lord. (12:10–19)

The writer of these verses admits that it is almost impossible to be at peace with certain people. The idea, though, is for us each to examine our *own* behavior. Are we working hard at living peacefully with the people in our church? In our workplace? In our own home? Are the qualities listed in this passage true of us?

Qualities That Encourage Relational Relief

From Genesis on, the Bible is full of relationships characterized by seasons of conflict. Adam and Eve . . . Cain and Abel . . . Jacob and Esau . . . Joseph and his brothers . . . Samuel and Saul . . . David and Absalom. Even Paul and Barnabas had their difficulties. No doubt you've had your share of relational struggles as well. By studying the qualities that people in successful relationships have in common, we can gain perspective on how to handle our own.

Insight

Another word for this quality might be *intuition*. It's the characteristic of being able to discern the undercurrents and nonverbal elements of a relationship. People who have it sense a problem before it arises. They know the things that make others react positively; they also know what makes them upset. They have the important ability to put themselves in other people's shoes.

Honesty

Honesty is having the courage to tell the truth about ourselves and others. It includes acknowledging our fears and inadequacies. It may also involve bringing another person's weaknesses to his or her attention. Remember Nathan's honesty in confronting David (2 Sam. 12)? That's what led to the king's confession (v. 13, compare Psalm 51). Paul's honesty about Peter's hypocrisy paved the way for Peter's future growth, as well as for the growth of their relationship (Gal. 2:11–14).

Firmness

A positive relationship is also characterized by firmness. Believers must firmly resolve to base their relationships upon biblical principles. Obedience to God's Word and His commands must come before our personal wants and desires in any relationship. Ironically, contrary to what the world says, making the decision to firmly stand by God's truth strengthens our relationships rather than destroying them.

Clarity

Last, people who relate well with others tend to have the ability to clarify difficult issues. They fight fairly, dealing with facts more than with feelings. They get at the heart of the problem rather than arguing over superficial, peripheral issues.

Conflict between Paul and the Corinthians

If you've kept up with this study so far, you know that Paul's relationship with the Corinthians was not exactly smooth sailing. Some of the conflict had come from outside the church, but some of it had come from within. Both of Paul's letters to the Corinthians were written at least in part to address these problems.

The problems coming from outside the church were largely cultural. Paul was Jewish; the Corinthians were Greek. Paul was intellectual by nature; the Corinthians tended to be more emotional. Paul thought theologically; the Corinthians were often sidetracked by worldly desires. Naturally, there was a collision of styles. And besides these differences, there were conflicts arising from the false teachers, who had damaged Paul's credibility.

From inside the church, there was the problem of cliques (1 Cor. 1:10–12). Some thought Paul was the best teacher; others liked Peter or Apollos. There were also the problems of carnality (3:1–9) and immorality (5:1–13). And, as we've seen before, some people were accusing Paul of hypocrisy (2 Cor. 10:10).

Exposing Wrong and Healing a Rift

Paul admits that he is far from perfect. He does not place blame; rather he seeks to restore peace in his relationship with the Corinthians. In his letter, he displays all four of the characteristics discussed earlier.

First, Paul shows *insight* when he *addresses the unspoken:*

> All this time you have been thinking that we are defending ourselves to you. Actually, it is in the sight of God that we have been speaking in Christ; and all for your upbuilding, beloved. (2 Cor. 12:19)

When you care about a relationship, you find yourself thinking about the other person even when he or she is not around. And you begin to understand his or her way of thinking. In the same way, Paul anticipates and addresses the Corinthians' objections before they arise, reaffirming his credibility in the eyes of God and reminding the Corinthians of his motive.

Next, Paul is *honest*—He *admits the unpleasant:*

> For I am afraid that perhaps when I come I may find you to be not what I wish and may be found by you to be not what you wish; that perhaps there will be strife, jealousy, angry tempers, disputes, slanders, gossip, arrogance, disturbances. (v. 20)

When's the last time you admitted to being afraid of something? Paul states his fear openly: "I'm afraid we may be disappointed in each other." And he goes on to specify the things he's worried may arise. He's concerned that there may be strife. And he thinks there could be jealousy — a sense of competition among the Christians. He also suspects arguments, slander, gossip, and prideful attitudes. Not much to look forward to!

In verse 21, Paul gets painfully direct:

> I am afraid that when I come again my God may humiliate me before you, and I may mourn over many of those who have sinned in the past and not repented of the impurity, immorality and sensuality which they have practiced.

In Paul's day, the very word *Corinthian* was a synonym for immorality. In fact, to *Corinthianize* meant "to fornicate." In this verse, Paul alludes to sexual misbehavior and uses terms that describe the downward spiral often involved. First, he uses the word *impurity.* This is a general word for sexual uncleanness, which occurs in the mind before any action occurs. The next word is stronger: *immorality.* This is the common term for adultery or fornication. The third word, *sensuality*, describes a quality of being so deeply involved in sexual immorality that there is no longer any sense of shame or guilt. This is what Paul is afraid he will find among the Corinthian believers.

In chapter 13, Paul demonstrates *firmness* when he *warns the unrepentant:*

> This is the third time I am coming to you. Every fact is to be confirmed by the testimony of two or three witnesses. I have previously said when present the second time, and though now absent I say in

80

advance to those who have sinned in the past and to all the rest as well, that if I come again I will not spare anyone. (vv. 1–2)

The time for gentle words is over. Paul is letting his readers know that he plans to clean house when he gets there.

In verses 3–4, we see Paul's *logic* as he *explains the unclear:*

Since you are seeking for proof of the Christ who speaks in me, and who is not weak toward you, but mighty in you. For indeed He was crucified because of weakness, yet He lives because of the power of God. For we also are weak in Him, yet we will live with Him because of the power of God directed toward you.

The Corinthians had criticized Paul for coming across strong in his letters, but being mild-mannered when he was with them. His gentle demeanor raised doubts about his claim to apostolic power and authority. He warns here that they will see a different side of him next time he visits. If they want to see the strength of Christ's hatred of sin, they'll see it—in Paul!

The Next Time You Face a Conflict

Conflicts creep up in our lives as surely as weeds crop up in a garden. When they do, here are three pieces of advice for hoeing them up.

First, *before blaming, attempt identification.* Put yourself in the other person's shoes. Try to imagine what he or she is thinking or feeling. Would you react the same way? Why or why not? What principles does the Word of God offer for dealing with your particular situation?

Second, *instead of arguing, ask questions.* What is the root of this conflict? Are my motives pure? Am I really seeking peace, or do I simply want to prove that I'm right? Am I being totally honest? Am I acknowledging my part of the problem?

Third, *rather than retaliating, pursue restoration.* Even if you have examined your heart and feel you have done nothing wrong, make sure the person knows that you care about your relationship with him or her. If you have wronged someone, humbly admit whatever fault is yours in the situation and seek to restore the relationship.

Remember this verse in Romans? "If possible, so far as it depends on you, be at peace with all men" (12:18).

Paul was not at peace with the Corinthians when he wrote this letter, but he was working toward that goal. He didn't toss the relationship with them aside, even though that would have been easier. Instead, he persistently pursued them, searching for ways to mend the rift that existed.

Living Insights

The conflict between Paul and his friends in Corinth may reflect a difficult relationship in your life right now. Are you experiencing pain similar to Paul's? Maybe you have a relationship in your life that needs mending. If so, describe the situation here.

_____

_____

_____

_____

_____

Now, practice the steps you learned in this lesson. First, put yourself in the other person's place. How do you think he or she views the situation? How do you think he or she is feeling right now?

_____

_____

_____

_____

_____

Second, ask yourself a few questions to gain perspective on the source of the conflict. Here are a few to get you started; you may need to add one or two of your own.

Have I really examined my own contribution to this conflict? What is it?

_____

_____

_____

_____

What is my real goal in this situation? To win? To restore the relationship? To prove a point?

_____

_____

_____

_____

Does this conflict go deeper than what appears on the surface? Is it masking underlying issues? If so, what are they?

_____

_____

_____

_____

Third, pursue reconciliation if it is at all possible. What steps can you take to ease the tension so that a productive conversation can take place? Commit to pray for the person every day, and continue to reach out to him or her in love.

_____

_____

_____

_____

If a conflict with another person has caused a rift between you and God, take time to restore that fellowship today. Ask Him to forgive you and to give you the strength to forgive any wrongs that may have been done to you. As you seek to restore your relationships, offer others the same grace that God has offered you.

Chapter 12

PASSING THE FAITH TEST
2 Corinthians 13:5–10

Socrates once said, "The unexamined life is not worth living."[1] But there's little danger of an unexamined life in society today! Modern life is full of tests for examination and evaluation, though they may not be the kind Socrates was talking about.

Just think of all the tests you've taken in your life. Tests in school. Driving tests. Medical tests. Occupational tests. Not one of these tests could be described as fun, yet every one of them has been valuable in some way. Some of them reveal aspects of who you are and what you know. Some of them give you needed information, represent milestones or offer you admittance to a new privilege or opportunity. Many tests require preparation, and often the knowledge gained in the process is the real benefit.

Other tests are personal, and it is sometimes hard to see their rewards until long afterward. Maybe you've lost a loved one or experienced a failure of some kind. Perhaps a dream has died or a financial disaster has devastated your world. Personal tests are the most difficult of all, and we don't always pass them with flying colors. But God allows tests and trials in our lives in order to make us more dependent on Him and to bring us to a point of greater spiritual maturity.

A Test That Many Never Take

There is one vital test that many people fail to take—the faith test. In 2 Corinthians 13, Paul recommends subjecting ourselves to this examination:

> Test yourselves to see if you are in the faith; examine yourselves! Or do you not recognize this about yourselves, that Jesus Christ is in you—unless indeed you fail the test? (v. 5)

Take note of the word *yourselves*. It appears three times in this brief verse. Not only is it emphasized by repetition; it is emphasized

---

1. Socrates, in *The Dialogues of Plato*, trans. Benjamin Jowett, in *Great Books of the Western World* (Chicago, Ill.: Encyclopedia Britannica, 1952), vol. 7, p. 210.

in the Greek translation by being placed at the beginning of the sentence. A more literal rendering might read: "You yourselves test . . . you yourselves prove . . . that Jesus Christ is in you." The reason for this emphasis? Only we ourselves can know whether Jesus is truly in us.

Three Criteria for Passing the Test

The faith test does not take into account church attendance. It doesn't give credit for prayer or Bible study or good works. There are three words in this verse that tell us the criteria for passing this exam: *test, prove,* and *recognize.*

The root of the first word, *test,* is *peirazō* in Greek. Take an objective look back over your life. Can you pinpoint a specific time when gave your life to Christ? Not a time when you were baptized. Not a time when you were dedicated by your parents. The test is whether or not there was a moment in time when you established a personal relationship with Jesus Christ and gave control of your life over to Him. If you can't remember, then you may never have taken that step of faith.

The root of the second word, *prove,* is *dokimazō* in Greek and is translated "examine." Think about this word in terms of an instructor and a student. The teacher must have tangible proof that his or her student has progressed through one grade before passing the student on to the next grade. Tests provide the proof that the student has successfully completed his or her work and learned the required material.

The root of the third word, *recognize,* is *epiginōskō.* It indicates full confidence and deep knowledge. Are you absolutely certain that Christ lives in you? All of us struggle with faith issues at times, but if you have truly accepted Christ, you should have a sense of peace and security concerning your salvation. If you do, you pass the test! But if you don't, the issue is most likely not yet settled.

This spiritual examination requires honesty and introspection. The purpose is not to see whether you pass or fail, but to answer life's most important question: Have you truly accepted Christ into your heart and life? If you have, some changes should have occurred in your life since that time. You should see evidence that Christ is working. Is your thought life different? Have your attitudes, goals, habits, and lifestyle changed to better reflect God's purposes for your life? If not, you may need to reexamine your heart.

Evidence of Faith

In verse 6, Paul brings himself and his fellow laborers into the picture:

> But I trust that you will realize that we ourselves do not fail the test.

Why does he do this? Remember, in the last several chapters, we've seen that there's been doubt about his credentials as an apostle. In this verse, he establishes that he has attained the first and most important criterion for teaching others about God—salvation. By talking about the faith test, he is not judging the Corinthians. He is asking them to examine themselves, just as he has done.

This is not a new idea in Scripture. Jesus Himself recommended it in Matthew 7:

> "Do not judge so that you will not be judged. For in the way you judge, you will be judged; and by your standard of measure, it will be measured to you. Why do you look at the speck that is in your brother's eye, but do not notice the log that is in your own eye? Or how can you say to your brother, 'Let me take the speck out of your eye,' and behold, the log is in your own eye? You hypocrite, first take the log out of your own eye, and then you will see clearly to take the speck out of your brother's eye." (vv. 1–5)

Jesus isn't suggesting that we should never use discernment to examine another person's life. He's just saying that we need to examine our own lives first! Later in the same chapter, He says:

> "Beware of the false prophets, who come to you in sheep's clothing, but inwardly are ravenous wolves. You will know them by their fruits. Grapes are not gathered from thorn bushes, nor figs from thistles, are they? So every good tree bears good fruit, but the bad tree bears bad fruit. A good tree cannot produce bad fruit, nor can a bad tree produce good fruit. Every tree that does not bear good fruit is cut down and thrown into the fire. So then, you will know them by their fruits." (vv. 15–20)

Just as we look for proof of faith in our own lives, the evidence of faith in others' lives will be easy to spot as well. Look at the way they live. Inspect their goals. You won't see perfection in them any more than you do in yourself; after all, sanctification is a process. But you should see signs of effort and increasing spiritual maturity, even if the areas they are working on might not be the ones you'd have chosen for them!

In 2 Corinthians 13:7, Paul sounds like a caring parent:

> Now we pray to God that you do no wrong; not that we ourselves may appear approved, but that you may do what is right, even though we may appear unapproved.

To some degree, Paul's reputation is on the line in the way his students in the faith behave—just as parents are often evaluated by how their children behave. But that is not Paul's concern. It's for their sake, not his, that he wants them to pass the test. Like all good teachers, he's committed to the pursuit of truth. And he's convinced that truth will ultimately win out:

> For we can do nothing against the truth, but only for the truth. (v. 8)

Like all good parents, Paul finds more joy in the accomplishments of his spiritual children than he does in his own:

> For we rejoice when we ourselves are weak but you are strong; this we also pray for, that you be made complete. (v. 9)

As we grow in maturity, we take fewer tests assigned by others, and we subject ourselves to more tests designed by ourselves. In verse 10, Paul urges the Corinthians to take that next step toward growing up. God had given Paul the authority to teach the Corinthians whatever they needed to know. In 2 Cor. 13:2, Paul suggested that his next visit may involve discipline. He asks the church to take care of those matters themselves so that when he comes, he can use his authority to encourage rather than discipline:

> For this reason I am writing these things while absent, so that when present I need not use severity, in accordance with the authority which the Lord gave me for building up and not for tearing down. (v. 10)

There's a lesson here to teachers as well as students in the faith. If you are in church leadership, remember your purpose! You're supposed to be lovingly herding sheep, not driving cattle! First Peter 5 gives us a picture of the way leadership should look:

> Therefore, I exhort the elders among you, as your fellow elder and witness of the sufferings of Christ, and a partaker also of the glory that is to be revealed, shepherd the flock of God among you, exercising oversight not under compulsion, but voluntarily, according to the will of God; and not for sordid gain, but with eagerness; nor yet as lording it over those allotted to your charge, but proving to be examples to the flock. (vv. 1–3)

The third book of John gives us an example of leadership run amok:

> I wrote something to the church; but Diotrephes, who loves to be first among them, does not accept what we say. For this reason, if I come, I will call attention to his deeds which he does, unjustly accusing us with wicked words; and not satisfied with this, he himself does not receive the brethren, either, and he forbids those who desire to do so and puts them out of the church. (vv. 9–10)

Don't miss this description of Diotrephes! He loved to be "first among them." But remember what Jesus said about this type of person in Matthew 19:30: "Many who are first will be last; and the last, first." When a person tries to usurp God's authority, he brings discredit to the faith.

A Suggested Process for Taking the Test

All of us, teachers and students alike, need to take the test of faith. Why? Because it will reveal the truth to us—and the truth will set us free (John 8:32).

Do you want to be free of doubt regarding your standing with God? Take the test. Do you want to be certain where you will spend eternity? Take the test. Once that issue is settled, you'll be free to grow to spiritual maturity. Satan would like nothing more than to convince that you're saved when you aren't. On the other hand, he'd love to make you think that you're *not* saved when you *are!* Take the test! Find out for sure! And then put the matter to rest.

Maybe you settled the issue of salvation long ago. If so, praise God for the joy of knowing Him personally and the blessings that heaven will bring!

But maybe you have never been quite certain of your status. Perhaps you have a gnawing sense of doubt regarding your relationship with God. Maybe you've gone to church all your life, but you do so with a sense of duty rather than joy. Perhaps your "faith" is really more like a moral code than a personal relationship. Maybe you sense an emptiness inside your soul that you've tried unsuccessfully to fill. Here is your opportunity to settle the issue once and for all.

First, *ask yourself the hard questions.* Do you feel alone, like you are still searching for a relationship with God but haven't found it yet? Are you the same person you have always been, or have your heart and your mind been changed by the power of God's grace and forgiveness? Are you relying on your own strength to make it through the day?

Second, *be sure your answers are honest.* You can fool other people, and you may even fool yourself for a period of time, but God knows your heart. He loves you just the way you are, and He desires to have a relationship with you. Be honest with yourself and with God.

Third, *review your answers.* If you answered no to any of the above questions and you want to accept Christ into your life, pray to Him right now. You may pray out loud or in the quietness of your heart. If you need help, you may use the prayer at the end of this chapter as a guide.

Fourth, *resist the temptation to rationalize.* Don't succumb to blaming your childhood, your mate, your job, or your circumstances for keeping you from accepting Christ or growing spiritually. All of these things certainly affect your life, but God wants to "bind up the brokenhearted, to proclaim liberty to the captives, and freedom to the prisoners" (Is. 61:1). You do not need to be bound by the things in your past or limited by the things in your present! The Lord wants to set you free . . . and the first step on the road to freedom is acknowledging your need for Him.

Finally, *embrace the truth.* If you have accepted Christ's free gift of forgiveness, you have passed the test of faith. Your "certificate of salvation" is one that never needs to be renewed or updated; it is good for eternity. Don't let anyone convince you that it can be lost! Once you have passed the faith test, you are a child of God's, and you will always be His. And that's good news!

 Living Insights

Establishing a personal relationship with God through His Son, Jesus Christ, is the most important decision you will ever make! Ask yourself the following questions if you are feeling unsure about your faith and your future:

- Have I ever specifically prayed to ask Jesus Christ to forgive my sins and come into my life?

- Do I see evidence of His work in my life? Are my attitudes any different now than they were in the past? Am I getting any easier to live with? Am I maturing in my understanding of God?

- If I were to die tonight, am I certain of where I would spend eternity?

- Are my thoughts and desires changing? Do I feel led to attend church, fellowship with other believers, pray, and read my Bible?

If you answered no to any or all of these questions, it is possible that you have never taken the step of establishing a personal relationship with God. An easy way to approach God in prayer is to remember the ABC's:

> I *accept* Jesus Christ as my Savior and as the Lord of my life.

> I *believe* that Jesus Christ is the Son of God, that He came to earth to die for my sins, and that He rose from the dead to offer me eternal life in heaven with Him.

> I *confess* that I am a sinner and that I have not lived up to God's standards of righteousness. I understand that my own merit and good works will not save me—only God's grace will.

If you want to establish a personal relationship with God right now, tell Him so! You may use this prayer as a guide, or use your own words:

"God, I admit that I am a sinner. I believe that Jesus is Your Son and that You sent Him to earth to die on the cross in my place. Thank you that He rose from the dead to save me from my sins and to offer me eternal life. Please come into my heart and my life right now and cleanse me from my sins. Help me to grow in my relationship with You. Help me to seek you and walk in your paths. Thank you for Your promise of salvation and eternal life in heaven with You. In the name of Jesus, Amen."

Once you have received Christ, it is important to find a church family where you can surround yourself with other believers. Once you have passed the faith test, your goal is to gain greater maturity in your walk with God. Praying, reading your Bible, and having fellowship with other Christians will help you in this growth process and provide encouragement for you. Congratulations! You've passed the test!

Chapter 13

A LOVE LETTER,
SEALED WITH A KISS

2 Corinthians 13:11–14

Public speaking is a lot like piloting an airplane. The part in the
middle is what's really important; it's what gets you where you're
going. But what people remember most is the takeoff and landing!

As any good speaker knows, if you want people to listen to you,
you have to grab their attention right at the beginning. And if you
want them to remember what you've said, you must have a strong
conclusion—one that summarizes the major points so they're not
forgotten.

Although we don't have the privilege of listening to Paul speak,
we can explore his use of attention-grabbing tactics in his letters. As
we study the last four verses of his second letter to the Corinthians,
we'll see him sum up his points and seal his letter with a kiss. But
before we do that, let's take time for a summary of where we've been.

An Encouraging Glance at the Truth Behind Us

Sandwiched between a brief introduction (1:1–2) and a short
conclusion (13:11–14) is the meat of 2 Corinthians. It can be divided
into three parts: chapters 1–7, chapters 8–9, and chapters 10–13.

In chapters 1–7, Paul deals with some critical concerns: suffering,
ministry, and godliness.[1] In chapters 8–9, he discusses gracious giving,
exhorting his readers to put their treasure where their hearts are.
And finally, in chapters 10–13, he presents his apostolic credentials,
reluctantly responding to the critics who have denied his authority.

Four Principles for Enduring Through Conflict

We can glean four principles from Paul's letter. First, *great people
are not immune to hard times*. In 2 Corinthians 4:7–18, Paul teaches
us that hard times are like God's anvil, where He shapes us into

---

1. Second Corinthians 1–7 is covered in the Bible study guide A *Ministry Anyone Could
Trust*, coauthored by Ken Gire, from the Bible-teaching ministry of Charles R. Swindoll
(Fullerton, Calif.: Insight for Living, 1989, revised, 2001).

the likeness of His Son, Jesus Christ. Right now, you may be feeling the flames of the furnace, wondering why you have to submit to the pain of being reshaped. Such difficult times will be the making of greatness if you'll let God carry out His plan.

Second, *hard times bring tensions that may seem confusing.* Times of struggle always seem to throw us for a loop. They seem to contradict the love God says He has for us. After all, when we love people, we do our best to protect them from heartache, don't we? Sometimes we despair over even the relatively minor upsets we face daily, let alone the kind of "afflictions, hardships, and distresses" Paul experienced (see 6:4b). When the really painful times come along, especially those involving loss . . . well, it's easy to wonder if God truly does love us.

Third, *such confusion is a needed reminder of our humanity.* Chapter 12 reminds us that when we are at our weakest, His strength is most evident in us. When life is easy, our need for God is often eclipsed by our lack of desire for Him. But the harder life gets, the more we have to rely on Him. And the more we rely on Him, the more clearly we see Him, and the more clearly His presence is seen in us.

Fourth, *difficulty plus humanity equals humility and maturity.* You'll never meet a humble person who hasn't experienced hurt, nor a mature person who hasn't known trials. Without the pain that God allows in our lives, we wouldn't grow up. And we wouldn't have the privilege of experiencing the power of God that lifts us up when we're too weak to stand.

A Concluding Look at Second Corinthians

At the end of chapter 13, we immediately see that Paul qualifies his closing remarks with the words: "Finally, brethren." Whoever else may have read and benefited from his earlier words, it's clear that these final few lines are intended for believers—Corinthian as well as current.

Some Practical Commands

Paul gives us six commands for how to live our lives:

> Finally, brethren, rejoice, be made complete, be comforted, be like-minded, live in peace; and the God of love and peace will be with you. Greet one another with a holy kiss. (vv. 11–12)

93

First, he says, be sure to *rejoice*. The Greek root for this term means "to be joyful." In other words, "Laugh more! Enjoy life!" Laughter doesn't just lighten our moods; it even has medical benefits, creating enzymes in the brain that actually reduce pain.[2] But we don't need doctors to tell us that! Solomon told us long ago that laughter was good not only for our spirits, but for our bodies as well:

> A joyful heart is good medicine,
> But a broken spirit dries up the bones. (Prov. 17:22)

Second, Paul tells us to *be made complete*. This comes from the Greek word *katartizō*, which means "restoration." This term suggests the idea of supplying what is missing to bring about full usefulness. It's used in reference to mending a torn net, setting a broken bone, equipping an army with supplies, or patching up anything that has been injured or damaged. The Revised Standard Version translates the phrase "Mend your ways."

Third, we're told to *be comforted*. The Greek term Paul uses here, *parakaleō*, can have one of several meanings. It's the same word John uses for the Holy Spirit, who comes alongside to help us. It can also be used in the context of instruction—to encourage, cheer, or console one another. But many scholars believe that Paul is using it in the exhortative sense. The New International Version translates it "Listen to my appeal."

Fourth, we are to *be like-minded*. Literally, this means "Think the same thing." Paul doesn't mean that we should become clones or automatons; he's simply asking us to have the same focus. In his letter to the church at Philippi, he emphasizes this idea again:

> Make my joy complete by being of the same mind, maintaining the same love, united in spirit, intent on one purpose. Do nothing from selfishness or empty conceit, but with humility of mind let each of you regard one another as more important than yourselves; do not merely look out for your own personal interests, but also for the interests of others. Have this attitude in yourselves which was also in Christ Jesus. (Phil. 2:2–5)

2. Bruce Larson, *There's a Lot More to Health than Not Being Sick* (Waco, Tex.: Word Books, 1981), p. 124.

Fifth, Paul asks us to *live in peace*. When we are like-minded, tuned in to Him, there's harmony. There's peace. We all play different notes, but they blend together to make a beautiful chord. Paul wants believers to live together in harmony, sending out music the rest of the world longs to hear.

Sixth, we're to *greet one another with a holy kiss*. This idea is a little shocking to us. Through the years, physical contact has come to have such sexual implications that we often shy away from it. It makes us uncomfortable. But what comfort and pleasure we're missing out on! Physical affection, when given and received with pure motives, is remarkably restorative. It need not be limited to close family members. When kept within appropriate bounds, expressions of affection and friendship ought to be a natural part of any gathering of believers.

Promises Worth Remembering

Paul leaves the Corinthians with some wonderful promises:

> The God of love and peace will be with you. All
> the saints greet you. (2 Cor. 13:11b, 13)

We can count on God's divine presence; He will always be with us. And we can also count on earthly companionship. The family of God is always ready to welcome one more!

Two Tips on Making the Message Stay with Us

Second Corinthians is so full of truth that it's hard for our minds to retain it all. But two tips will help reinforce Paul's overall message.

First, *release the love of God, wherever you may be*. Paul's letter was written with the purpose of tugging the Corinthians' wayward hearts back to God. There's nothing more magnetic than God's love, so let it show.

Second, *remember the God of love, whatever may happen to you*. God is there with you in all your struggles and all your pain. He loves you with such incredible depth that He gave His Son so that you might spend eternity with Him. It's easy to remember Him when everything's going well. But if you can remember His love when darkness overcomes you, the message of 2 Corinthians will have hit home.

Paul closes his letter with a benediction that has been repeated for centuries:

> The grace of the Lord Jesus Christ, and the love of God, and the fellowship of the Holy Spirit, be with you all. (v. 14)

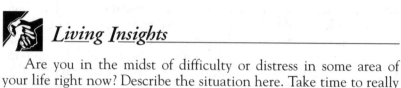 *Living Insights*

Are you in the midst of difficulty or distress in some area of your life right now? Describe the situation here. Take time to really pour out the way you feel about it.

_____

_____

_____

_____

_____

_____

_____

_____

_____

Sometimes it helps to read the words of someone who has felt the way you feel. Open your Bible to Lamentations 3 and read the first 20 verses. Can you relate to Jeremiah? Something happens in verses 21–33. Read on, and write down what changed. Note that verse 21 is pivotal.

_____

_____

_____

_____

Why do you think Jeremiah was able to praise God when he was clearly experiencing heartbreaking times?

_____

_____

_____

_____

_____

Reread verses 22–23. In what ways have the Lord's compassions been new to you every morning?

_____

_____

_____

_____

At times, all of us fail to see God's hand at work in our lives. What might be keeping you from recognizing God's blessings in your life?

_____

_____

_____

_____

Take time now to ask God to clear your mind and heart of the things that block your view of Him. Be encouraged by this: if God chooses not to remove the difficulties from your path, He will give you the grace to endure them. And in doing so, He will present you with a view of Himself that you have never seen. Climbing the mountains in your life may be a struggle, but the view from the top will be spectacular!

Chapter 14

HEART TROUBLE
Isaiah 29:13–16, Matthew 15:1–20

Have you ever thought much about your heart? If you've ever had cardiac problems, you've probably given it a lot of thought. That little fist-sized muscle beats more than a hundred thousand times a day, sending oxygen through a hundred thousand miles of arteries, veins, and capillaries in our bodies. In just one hour, the heart does enough work to lift a five-ton weight a foot off the ground. When it stops working, so does everything else.

God says a lot about the heart in His Word. If we were to look up *heart* in an exhaustive Bible concordance, we would find more than a thousand references. Isn't it interesting that God chooses a term so vital to physical life when referring to spiritual life? Healthy hearts are described in the Bible as having integrity, purity, compassion, praise, joy, and wisdom. Diseased hearts, on the other hand, are described as hardened, obstinate, divided, deceptive, proud, and blind.

The Bible uses the word *heart* to represent our whole inner being—the seat of the mind, soul, spirit, and emotions. That's why Solomon exhorts us in the book of Proverbs:

> Watch over your heart with all diligence,
> For from it flow the springs of life. (4:23)

God Sees Our Hearts

We often evaluate people according to their appearance. But God sees past our physical exterior into the depth of our souls. Read this verse from 1 Samuel:

> The Lord said to Samuel, "Do not look at his appearance or at the height of his stature, because I have rejected him; for God sees not as man sees, for man looks at the outward appearance, but the Lord looks at the heart." (16:7)

In Hebrew, the original language of this text, the word for *heart* is *lebab*. It "not only includes the motives, feelings, affections, and

This message was not part of the original series but is compatible with it.

desires, but also the will, the aims, the principles, the thoughts, and the intellect."[1]

In Greek, the word for *heart* is *kardia*, from which we get our word *cardiology*. Gerhard Kittel describes the term this way:

> The heart is the centre of the inner life of man and the source or seat of all the forces and functions of soul and spirit. . . . Thus *[kardia]* comes to stand for the whole of the inner being of man in contrast to his external side. . . . The heart is supremely the one centre in man to which God turns, in which the religious life is rooted, which determines moral conduct.[2]

God's Word has the ability to convict and change our hearts. As Hebrews 4:12 states:

> For the Word of God is living and active and sharper than any two-edged sword, and piercing as far as the division of soul and spirit, of both joints and marrow, and able to judge the thoughts and intentions of the heart.

We're going to do a biblical assessment of the condition of our hearts using one passage from the Old Testament and one from the New.

Principles from the Old Testament

God gave the prophet Isaiah a vision of woe concerning Jerusalem and His wayward people:

> "Woe to the rebellious children," declares the Lord,
> "Who execute a plan, but not Mine!" (Isaiah 30:1)

The people's hearts were far from God. They were acting upon their own desires and not upon God's commandments and principles. So Isaiah got to the very "heart" of the problem:

> Then the Lord said,
> "Because this people draw near with their words

1. Robert Baker Girdlestone, *Synonyms of the Old Testament* (1897; reproduction, Grand Rapids, Mich.: William B. Eerdmans Publishing Co., n.d.), p. 65.

2. Gerhard Kittel, ed., *Theological Dictionary of the New Testament*, trans. Geoffrey W. Bromiley (Grand Rapids, Mich.: William B. Eerdmans Publishing Co., 1965), vol. 3, pp. 611–12.

And honor Me with their lip service,
But they remove their hearts far from Me,
And their reverence for Me consists of tradition
learned by rote,
Therefore behold, I will once again deal marvelously
with this people, wondrously marvelous;
And the wisdom of their wise men will perish,
And the discernment of their discerning men will
be concealed." (29: 13–14)

The people were going through the motions. There was no substance to their worship, no real love or penitence in their prayers. This is the first symptom of heart trouble—*the spiritual life becomes superficial and routine*. Verse 15 describes the second symptom:

Woe to those who deeply hide their plans from the
Lord,
And whose deeds are done in a dark place,
And they say, "Who sees us?" or "Who knows us?"

This is a picture of people who are separated from God, cut off from any life-changing contact with Him, trying to hide their deeds in darkness. Sound familiar? When there's heart trouble, *we often try to operate in secrecy from God*—even though we know deep down that He sees everything! We don't want our sinful activities to be brought to light.

In the next verse, Isaiah diagnoses another "heart problem":

You turn things around!
Shall the potter be considered as equal with the clay,
That what is made would say to its maker, "He did
not make me";
Or what is formed say to him who formed it, "He
has no understanding"? (v. 16)

The people were treating God as their equal, as though He were just another person. They acted as though they could do whatever they pleased without suffering any consequences. They failed to realize that the Potter is sovereign over the clay.

When we have heart trouble, *we sometimes tend to see God as no more important than ourselves*. We often fail to consider Him in the choices we make; we do as we please without considering the consequences. But God is the Sovereign Potter. He has control over the details of our lives. And more importantly, He loves us intimately—and He desires to shape the clay of our hearts and lives into a beautiful vessel that can be used by Him.

Principles from the New Testament

Physical heart trouble is often hereditary. Spiritual heart trouble, too, is often passed down from generation to generation. Just as this disease afflicted the Old Testament Jews, so it was the number one killer of spiritual life at the time of Christ.

Jesus describes the lives of some extremely important religious leaders who looked holy on the outside but who were hypocrites underneath. In Matthew 15, we see Jesus having a run-in with them:

> Then some Pharisees and scribes came to Jesus from Jerusalem and said, "Why do Your disciples break the tradition of the elders? For they do not wash their hands when they eat bread." And He answered and said to them, "Why do you yourselves transgress the commandment of God for the sake of your tradition? For God said, 'Honor your father and mother,' and, 'He who speaks evil of father or mother is to be put to death.' But you say, 'Whoever says to his father or mother, "Whatever I have that would help you has been given to God," he is not to honor his father or his mother.' And by this you invalidated the word of God for the sake of your tradition." (vv. 1–6)

The word *invalidated* in verse 6 comes from the Greek root *kuros*, which means "authority." Here the term is *akuroo*, meaning "non-authority." Jesus was telling them that by putting their traditions on equal footing with Scripture, they were usurping the authority of God's Word. This illustrates the fourth symptom of heart trouble: *caring more about external tradition than about God's Word.*

Jesus' words get stronger in verses 7–9, and He quotes for them the very passage we just read in Isaiah:

> "You hypocrites, rightly did Isaiah prophesy of you:
> 'This people honors Me with their lips,
> But their heart is far away from Me.
> But in vain do they worship Me,
> Teaching as doctrines the precepts of men.'"

It's clear from this passage that love is not always meek. Jesus uses some strong words here—He calls the religious leaders hypocrites! These Pharisees were suffering from the fifth symptom of heart trouble: *practicing hypocrisy rather than modeling authenticity.*

In the surrounding verses, Jesus diagnoses their problem:

> "Hear, and understand. It is not what enters into the mouth that defiles the man, but what proceeds out of the mouth, this defiles the man. . . . But the things that proceed out of the mouth come from the heart, and those defile the man. For out of the heart come evil thoughts, murders, adulteries, fornications, thefts, false witness, slanders. These are the things which defile the man; but to eat with unwashed hands does not defile the man." (Matt. 15:10b–11, 18–20)

The Pharisees were focusing on external rituals while trying to hide their evil thoughts and sinful actions. They had heart trouble. No doubt about it.

A Look Inside Your Heart

Here's some good news: Heart trouble doesn't have to be fatal! In fact, if you have a relationship with Christ, eternal life is yours forever. But a heart problem can certainly cripple your spiritual life. It keeps you from living the abundant life God has planned for you and from participating in His activities in this world. And worse, it saddens the heart of God.

 Living Insights

What is the condition of your heart? Take a few minutes to answer the following questions and see whether it is in good working condition.

Has my worship become dry and formal?	*Yes*	*No*
Has my prayer life become rote and meaningless?	*Yes*	*No*
Does God seem distant from me as I go about my daily life?	*Yes*	*No*
Do I wonder whether He really knows what I do and think?	*Yes*	*No*

Do I find myself preoccupied with worldly things to the exclusion of spiritual things? Are my desires in line with God's desires?	Yes	No
Has acceptance by others become more important to me than God's truth in my life?	Yes	No
Do I tolerate, or even cultivate, evil in my life?	Yes	No

Did you discover that you had heart trouble as you answered the questions? If so, which areas were the main trouble spots for you? Describe your symptoms here.

_____

_____

_____

_____

_____

_____

_____

It's unlikely you are doing this exercise, or even participating in this study, if you are so far from God as to not care about the state of your heart. But Satan is always looking for a weak spot to attack—and He is usually pretty sly about it. His assaults are insidious and gradual. Slowly, over time, he dulls your senses so that God seems far away, unrelated to your daily life. Little by little, he distracts you from studying the Bible so that you forget what's important to God. He helps your mind to wander during services, so that your worship is distracted and insincere.

Can you think of any habits that may have crept in over time to weaken your spiritual condition?

_____

_____

_____

_____

_____

_____

_____

_____

How might you go about correcting these areas of weakness? Choose one or two of the most significant ones, and write your "prescription" for change here.

_____

_____

_____

_____

_____

_____

_____

Your heart may be in great condition—or it may be in need of an operation. Just remember: Christ came to heal the sick, not the healthy. He knows you're fallible. He knows how easy it is to lose sight of Him. He knows that our hearts are disastrously susceptible to disease. No matter how corrupt your heart has become, He can make it clean (Ps. 51:10a). No matter how dry and hardened, He can make it warm and responsive (Ps. 51:12). Ask Him to heal your heart!

BOOKS FOR PROBING FURTHER

W e have reached the end of our journey through 2 Corinthians. And what a journey it has been! In this latter half of Paul's letter, we have encountered such timely and relevant topics as financial responsibility, spiritual warfare, false ministries, God's sovereignty, pain, relationships, and our need for spiritual self-examination.

We hope that this journey has given you the opportunity to expand your horizons and experience some life-changing views along the way. To provide you with the opportunity to explore these topics more deeply, we recommend the following books. As you continue your travels through the Christian life, we hope these books will make the road more smooth and the journey more refreshing.

Barna, George. *Turning Vision into Action*. Ventura, Calif.: Gospel Light Publications, 1997.

Blue, Ron. *Generous Living*. Grand Rapids, Mich.: Zondervan Publishing House, 1997.

———. *Master Your Money*. Nashville, Tenn.: Thomas Nelson Publishers, 1997.

———. *Taming the Money Monster*. Colorado Springs, Colo.: Focus on the Family Publishers, 2000.

Bridges, Jerry. *Transforming Grace*. Colorado Springs, Colo.: NavPress, 1993.

———. *Trusting God*. Colorado Springs, Colo.: NavPress, 1988.

Brown, Daniel Alan. *The Other Side of Pastoral Ministry*. Grand Rapids, Mich.: Zondervan Publishing House, 1996.

Bubeck, Mark. *Preparing for Battle: A Spiritual Warfare Workbook*. Chicago, Ill.: Moody Press, 1999.

Dawson, John. *Healing America's Wounds*. Ventura, Calif.: Regal Books, 1994.

Gangel, Kenn. *Coaching Ministry Teams*. Nashville, Tenn.: Word Publishing, 2000.

————. *Ministering to Today's Adults*. Nashville, Tenn.: Word Publishing, 1999.

Gordon, Ruth. *Children of Darkness*. (This book is a true account of Gordon's experiences with the Children of God cult.) Wheaton, Ill.: Tyndale House Publishers, 1988.

Hendricks, Howard. *Teaching to Change Lives*. Portland, Ore.: Multnomah Press, 1987.

Logan, Jim. *Reclaiming Surrendered Ground: Protecting Your Family from Spiritual Attacks*. Chicago, Ill.: Moody Press, 1995.

Lucado, Max. *In the Grip of Grace*. Thomas Nelson Publishers, 1999.

Piper, John. *Desiring God*. Sisters, Ore.: Multnomah Books, 1996.

Spurgeon, Charles Haddon. *Spiritual Warfare in a Believer's Life*. Emerald Books, 1996.

Swindoll, Charles. *The Grace Awakening*. Dallas, Texas: Word Publishing, 1996.

Some of the books listed may be out of print and available only through a library. For those currently available, please contact your local Christian bookstore. Books by Charles R. Swindoll may be obtained through the Insight for Living Resource Center, as well as many books by other authors. Just call the IFL office that serves you.

Insight for Living also has Bible study guides available on many books of the Bible as well as on a variety of topics, Bible characters, and contemporary issues. For more information, see the ordering instructions that follow and contact the office that serves you.

ORDERING INFORMATION

A MINISTER EVERYONE WOULD RESPECT

If you would like to order additional Bible study guides, purchase the audiocassette series that accompanies this guide, or request our product catalogs, please contact the office that serves you.

United States and International locations:

Insight for Living
Post Office Box 269000
Plano, TX 75026-9000

1-800-772-8888, 24 hours a day, seven days a week (U.S. contacts) International constituents may contact the U.S. office through mail queries.

Canada:

Insight for Living Ministries
Post Office Box 2510
Vancouver, BC, Canada V6B 3W7

1-800-663-7639, 24 hours a day, seven days a week
InfoCanada@insight.org

Australia:

Insight for Living, Inc.
20 Albert Street
Blackburn, VIC 3130, Australia

Toll-free 1800 772 888 or (03) 9877-4277, 8:30 A.M. to 5:00 P.M., Monday to Friday
iflaus@insight.org

World Wide Web:
www.insight.org

Bible Study Guide Subscription Program

Bible study guide subscriptions are available. Please call or write the office nearest you to find out how you can receive our Bible study guides on a regular basis.